Fuck Off!
I'm Coloring

Volume One

Swearing N' Coloring

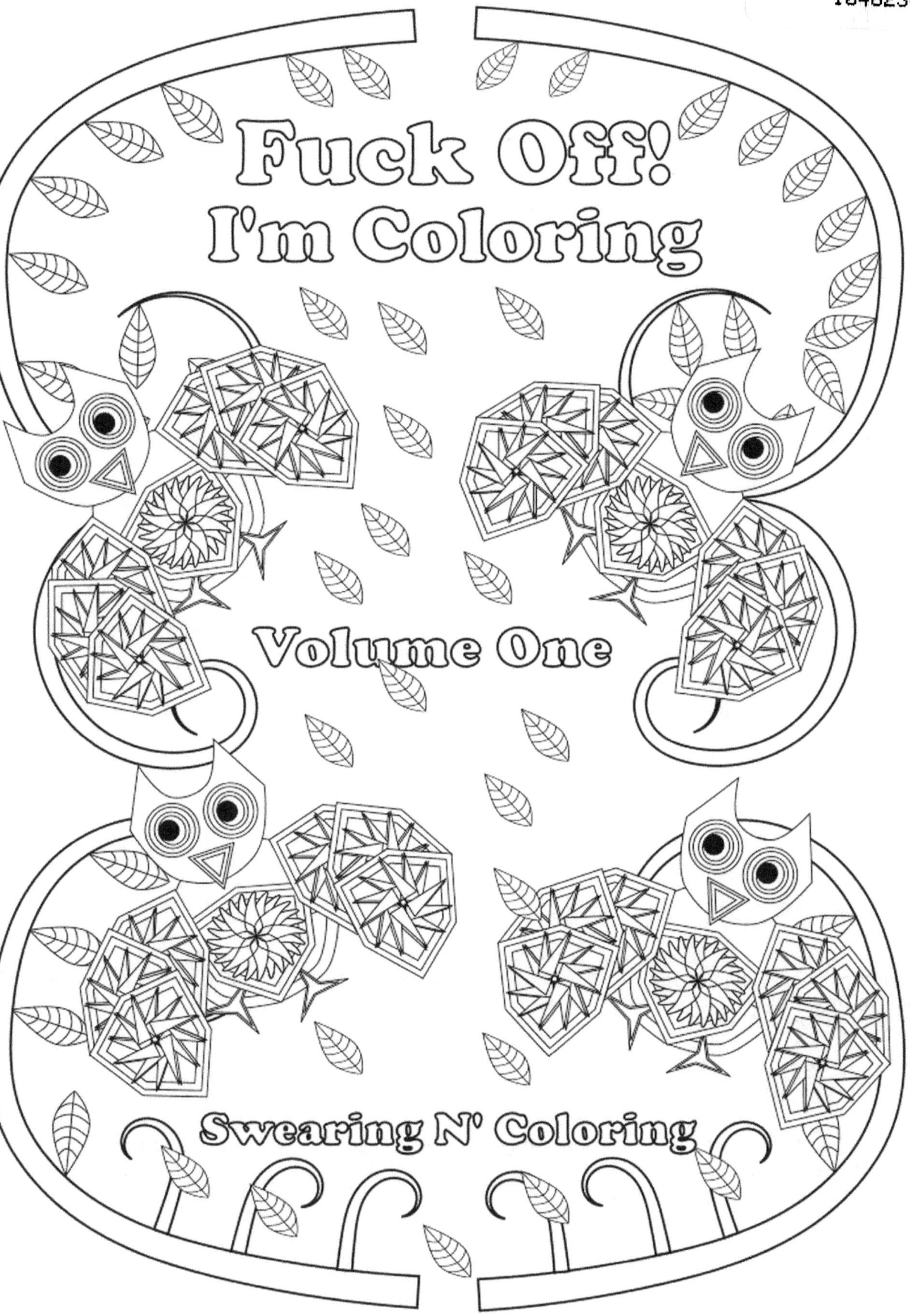

F*ck Off! I'm Coloring: Bitchin' Blue Cover Edition: A Swear Word Adult Coloring Book with Owls, Flowers, and other Relaxing Designs
Copyright 2016 by Don Cummings

ISBN-13: 978-1533512307
ISBN-10: 1533512302

First Edition 2016

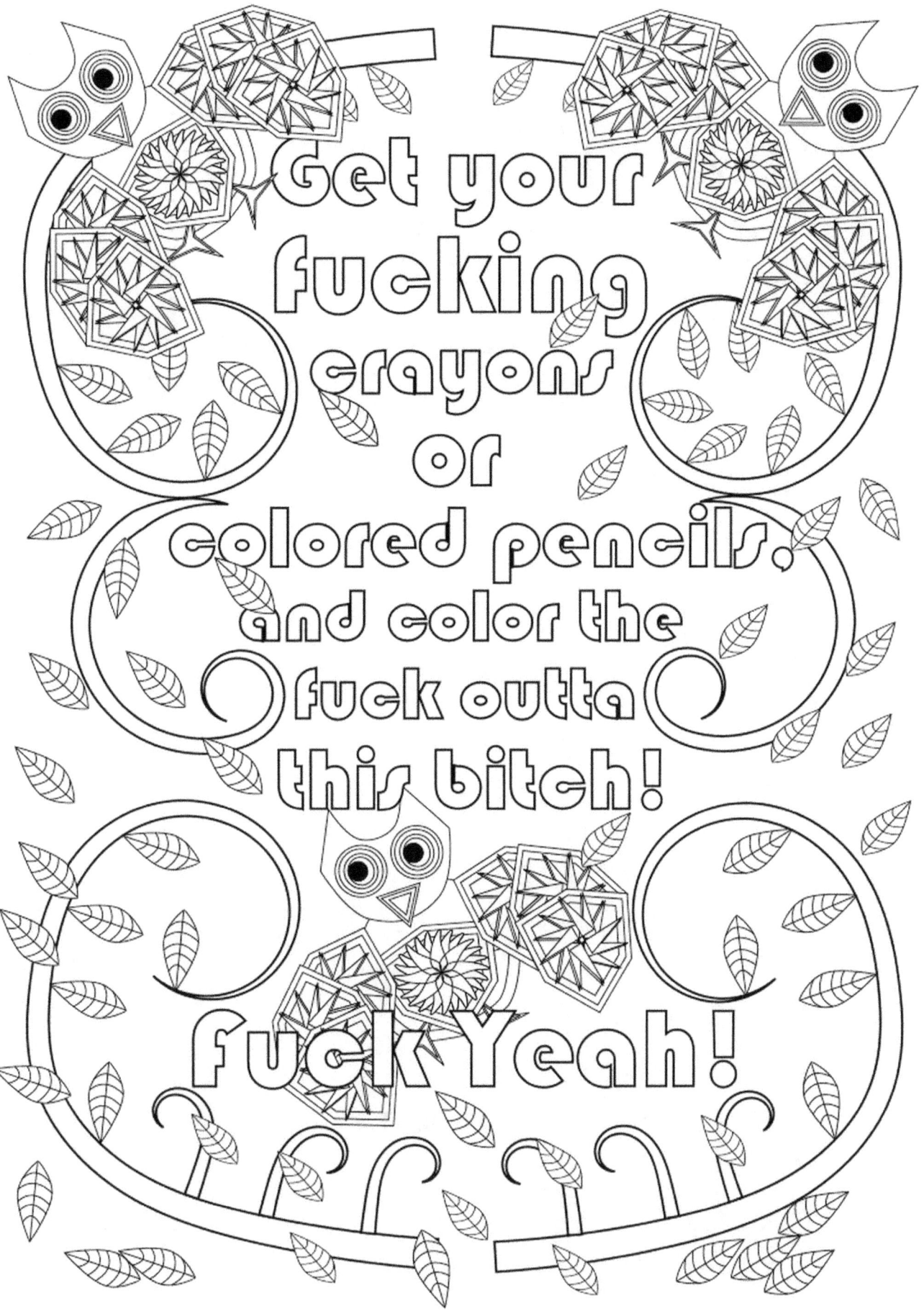

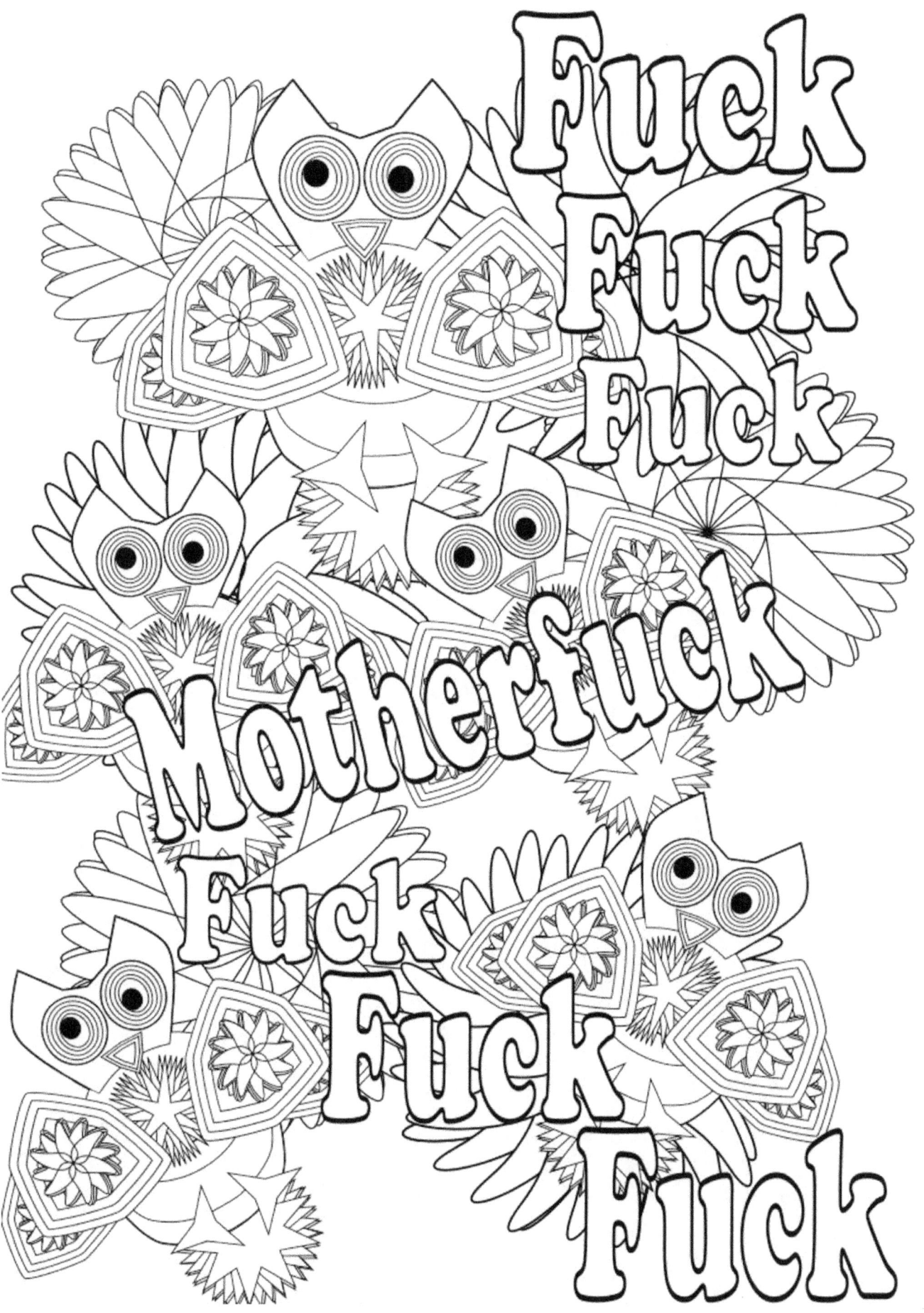

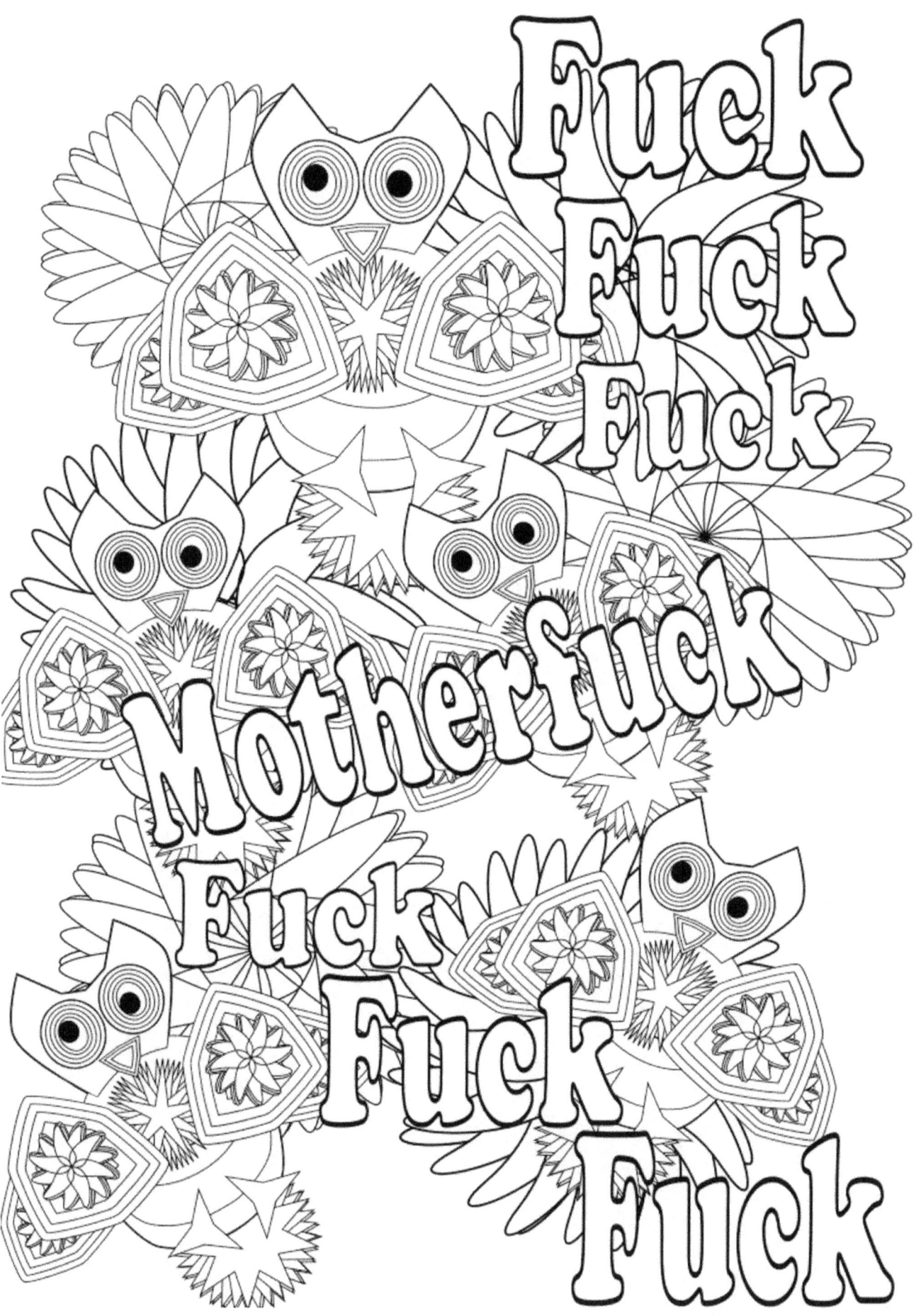

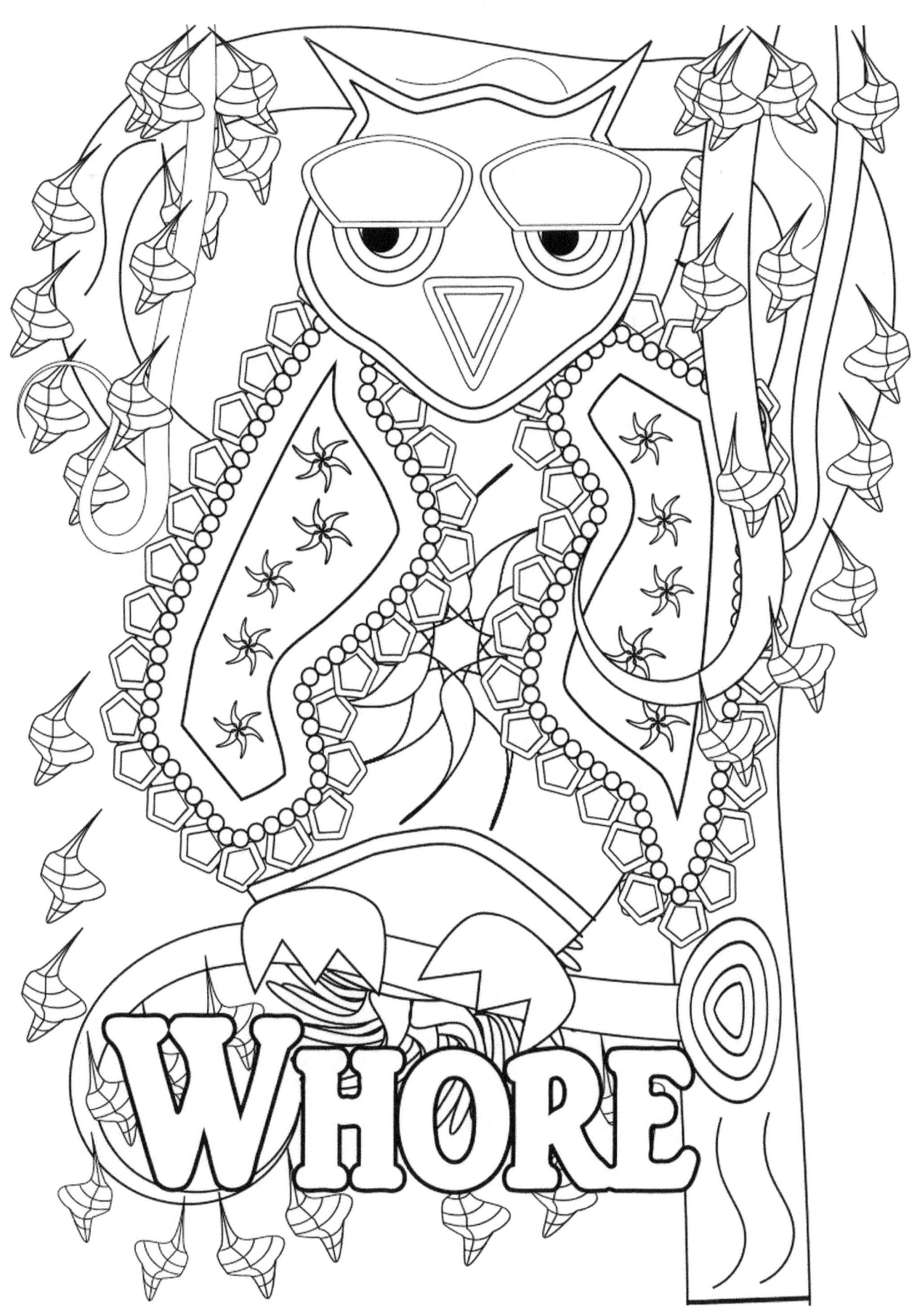

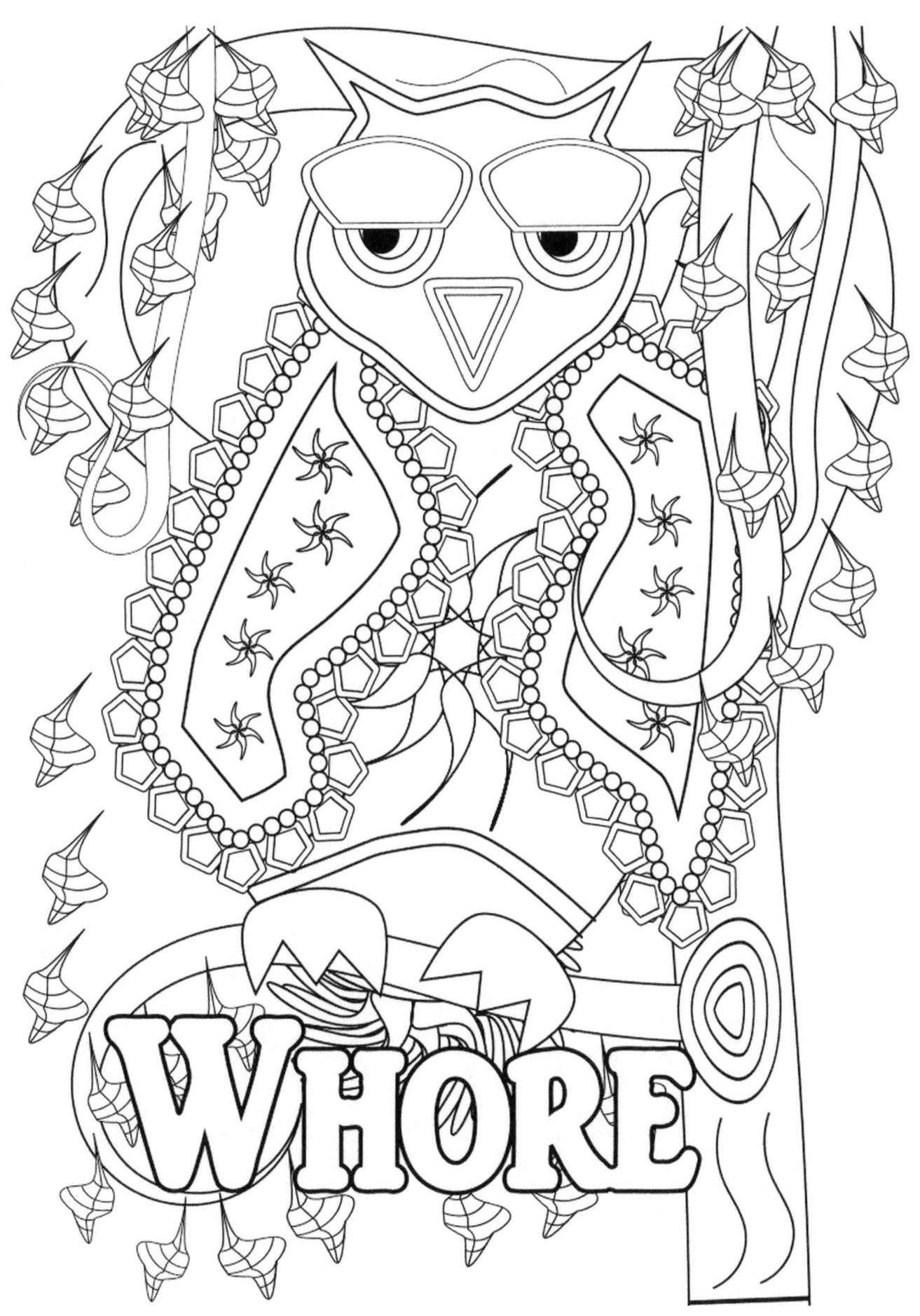

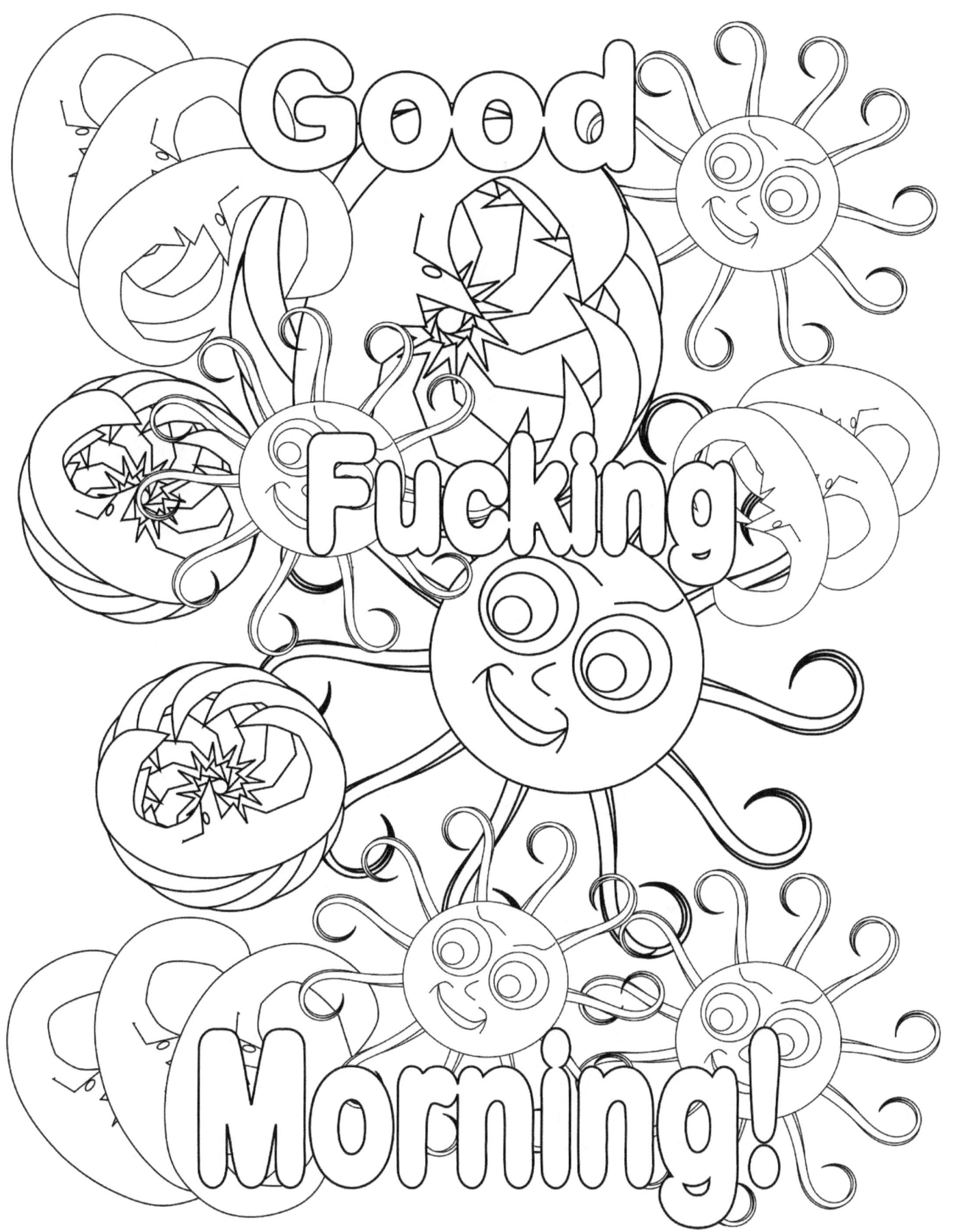

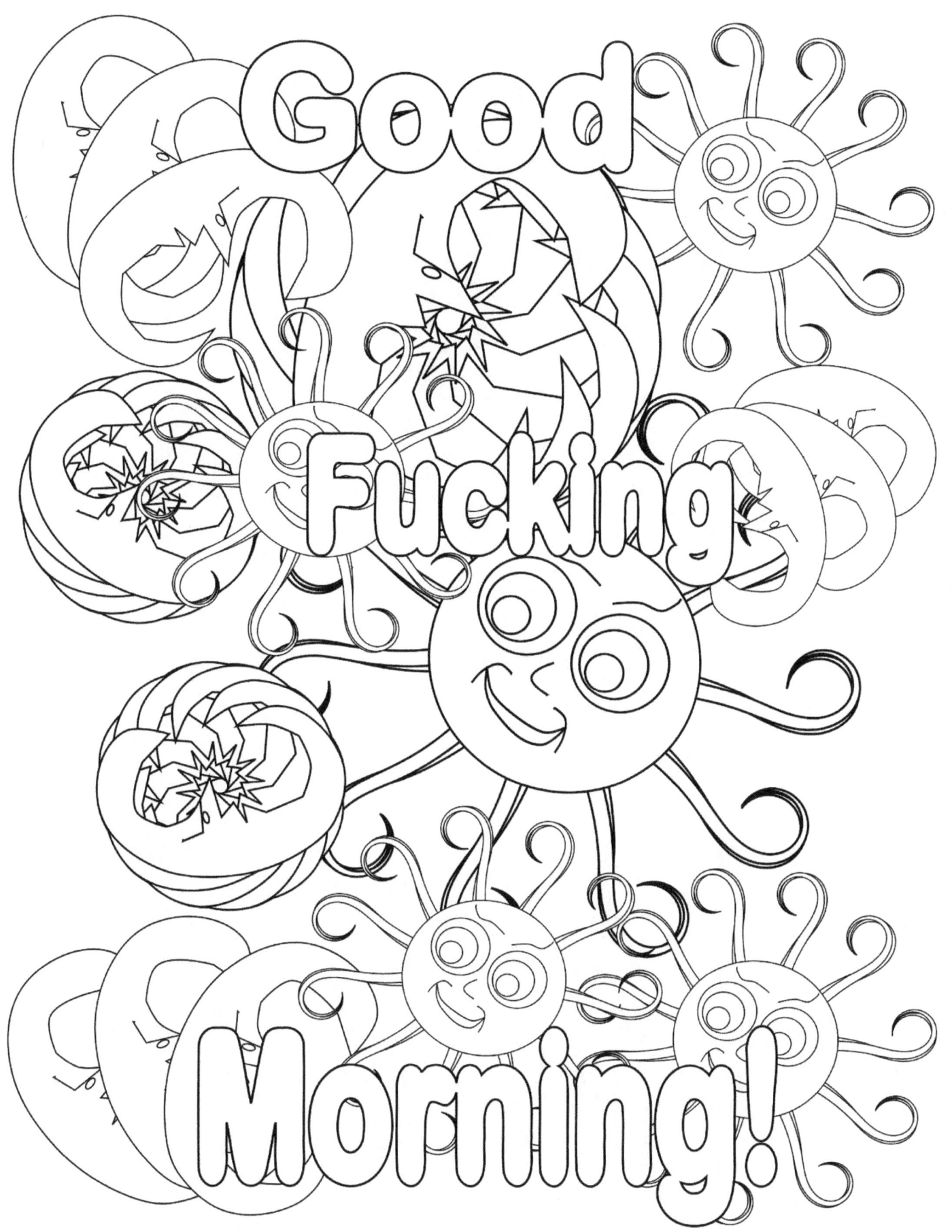

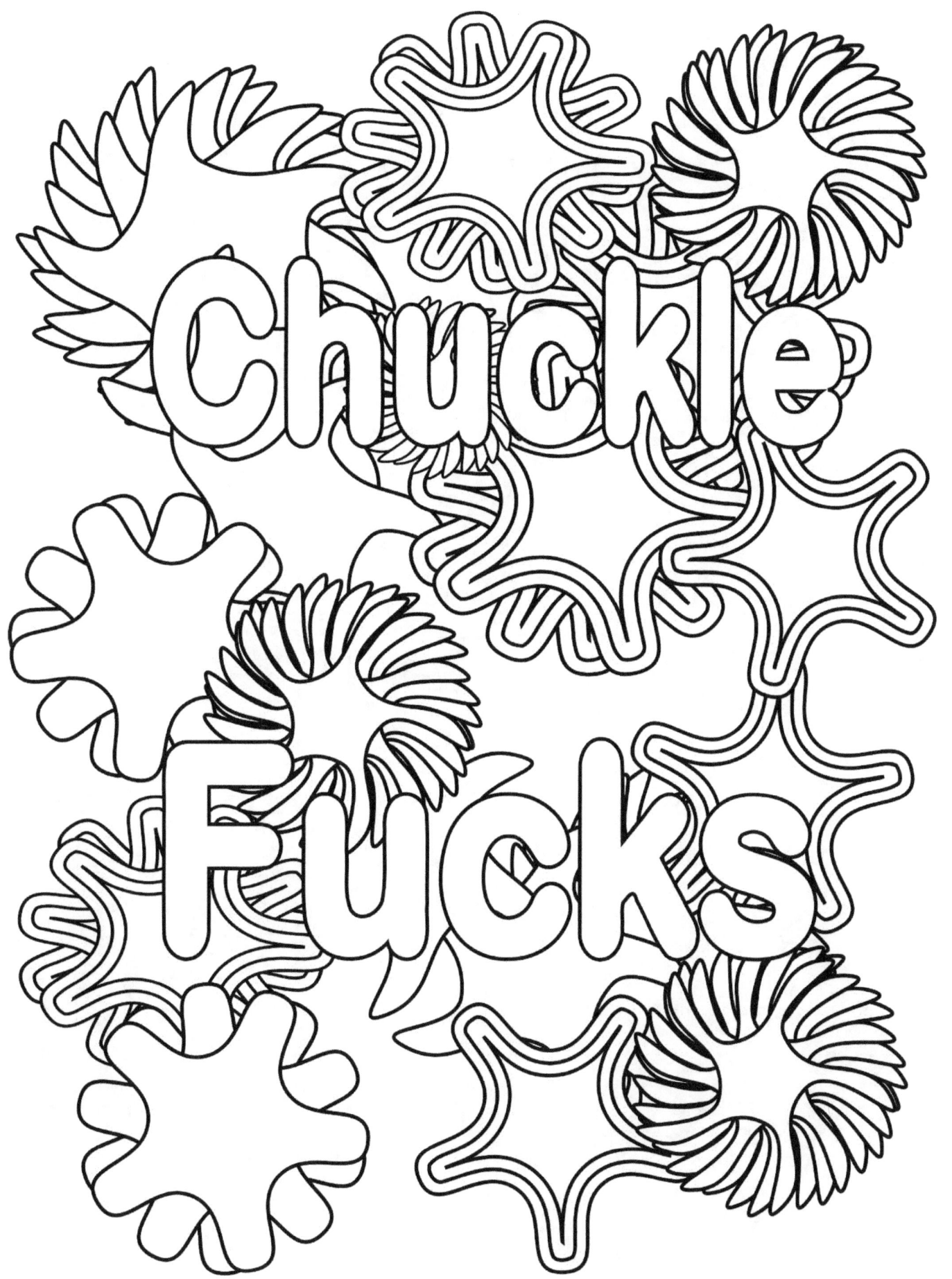

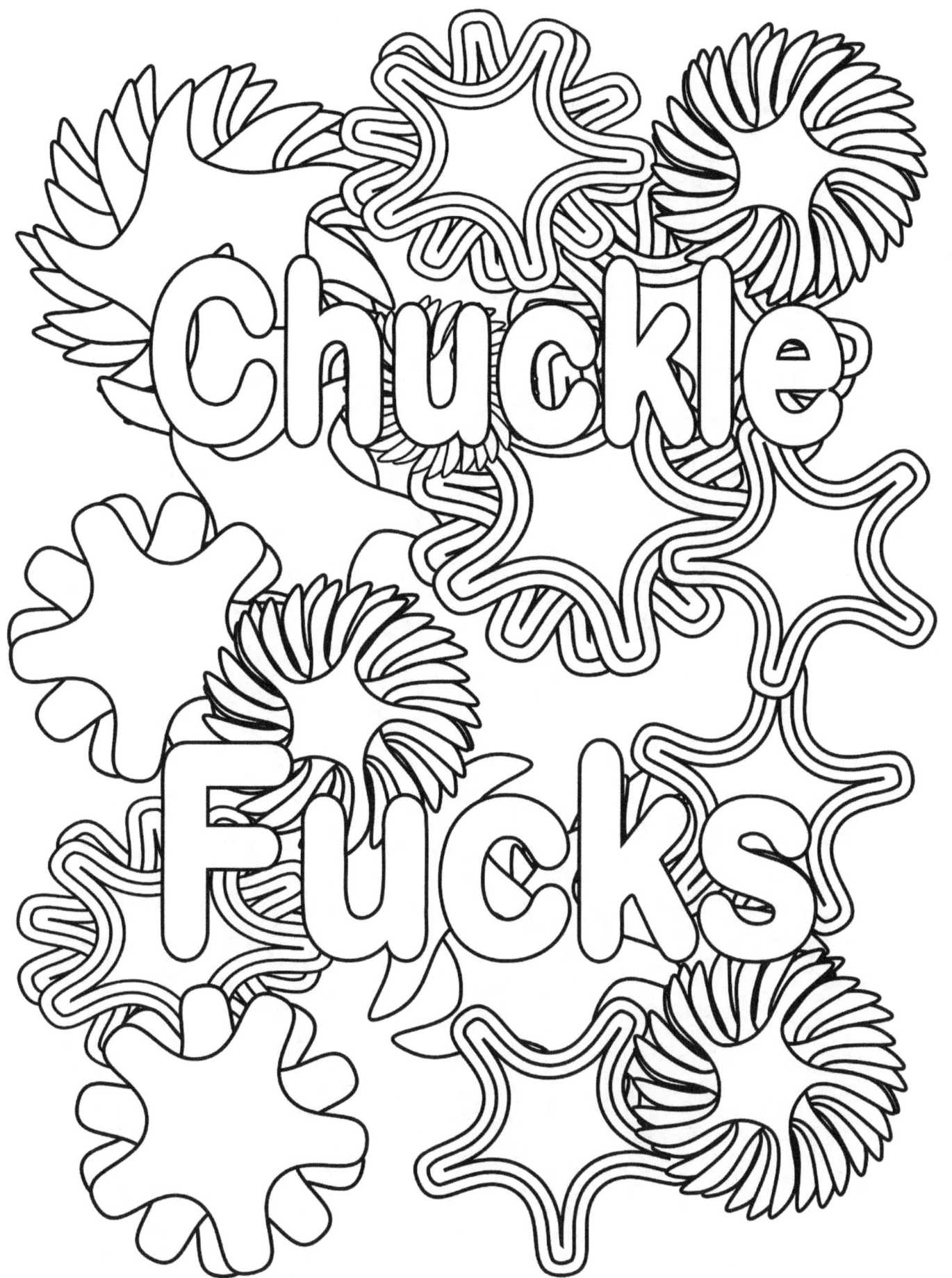

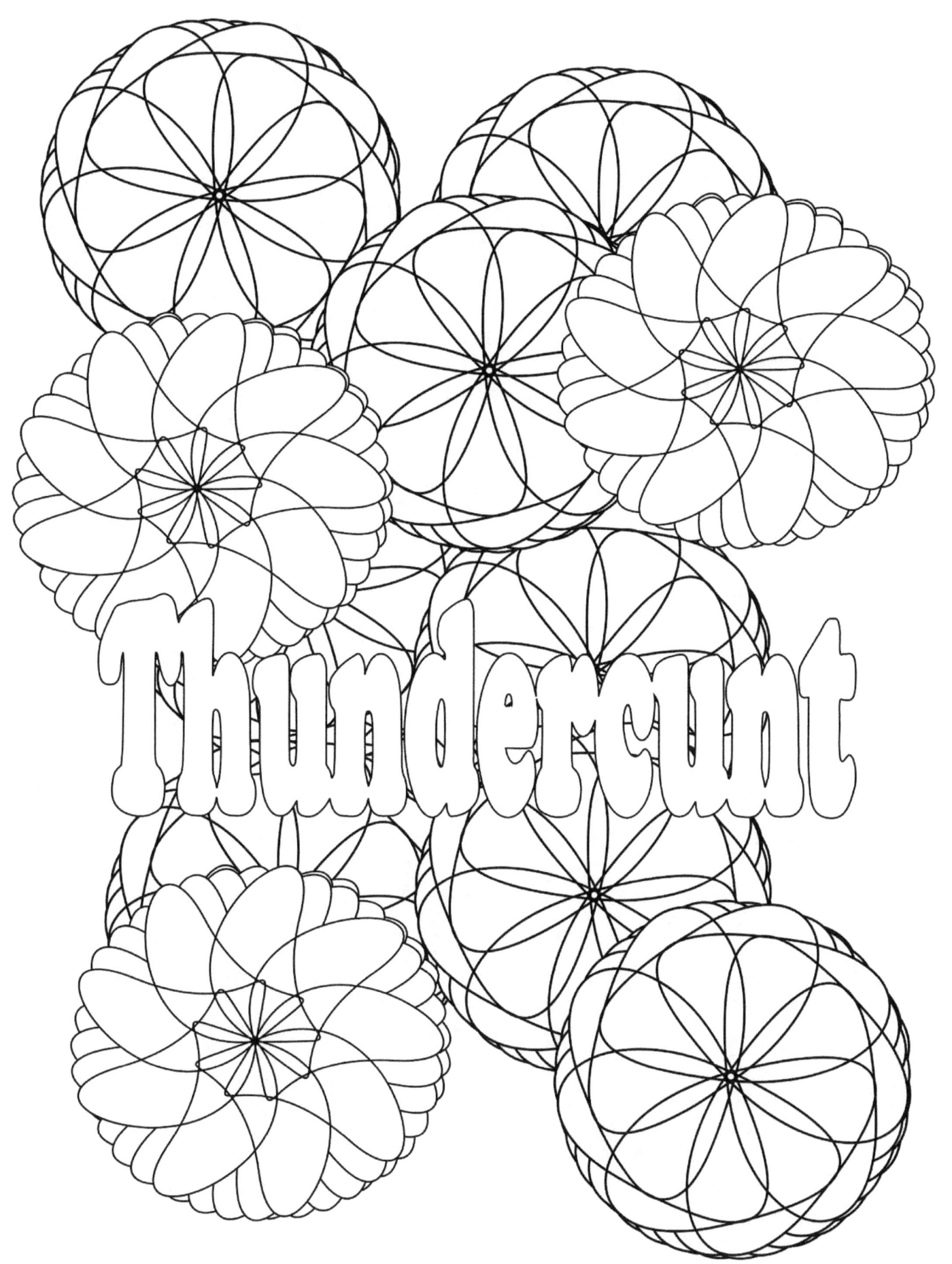

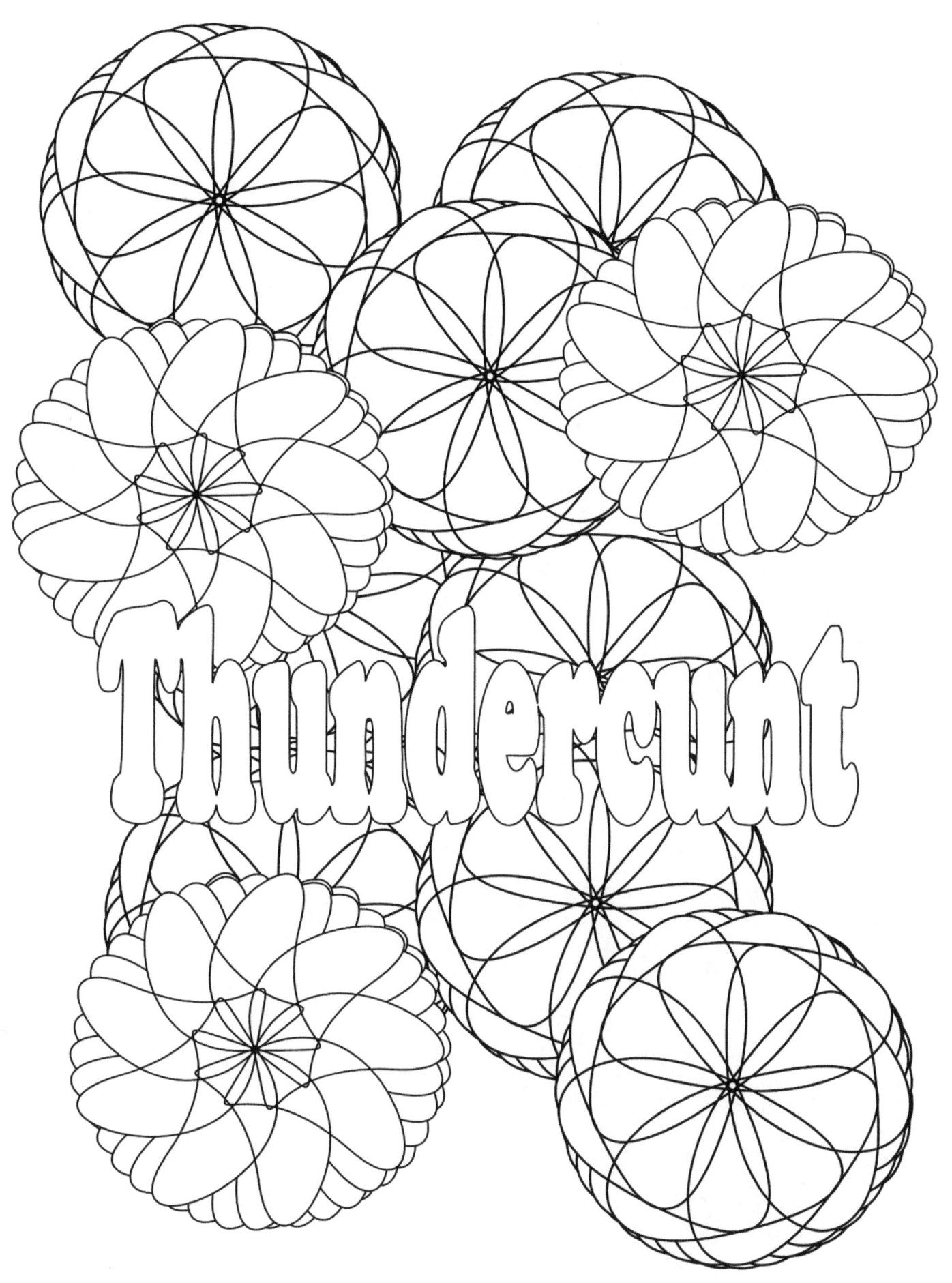

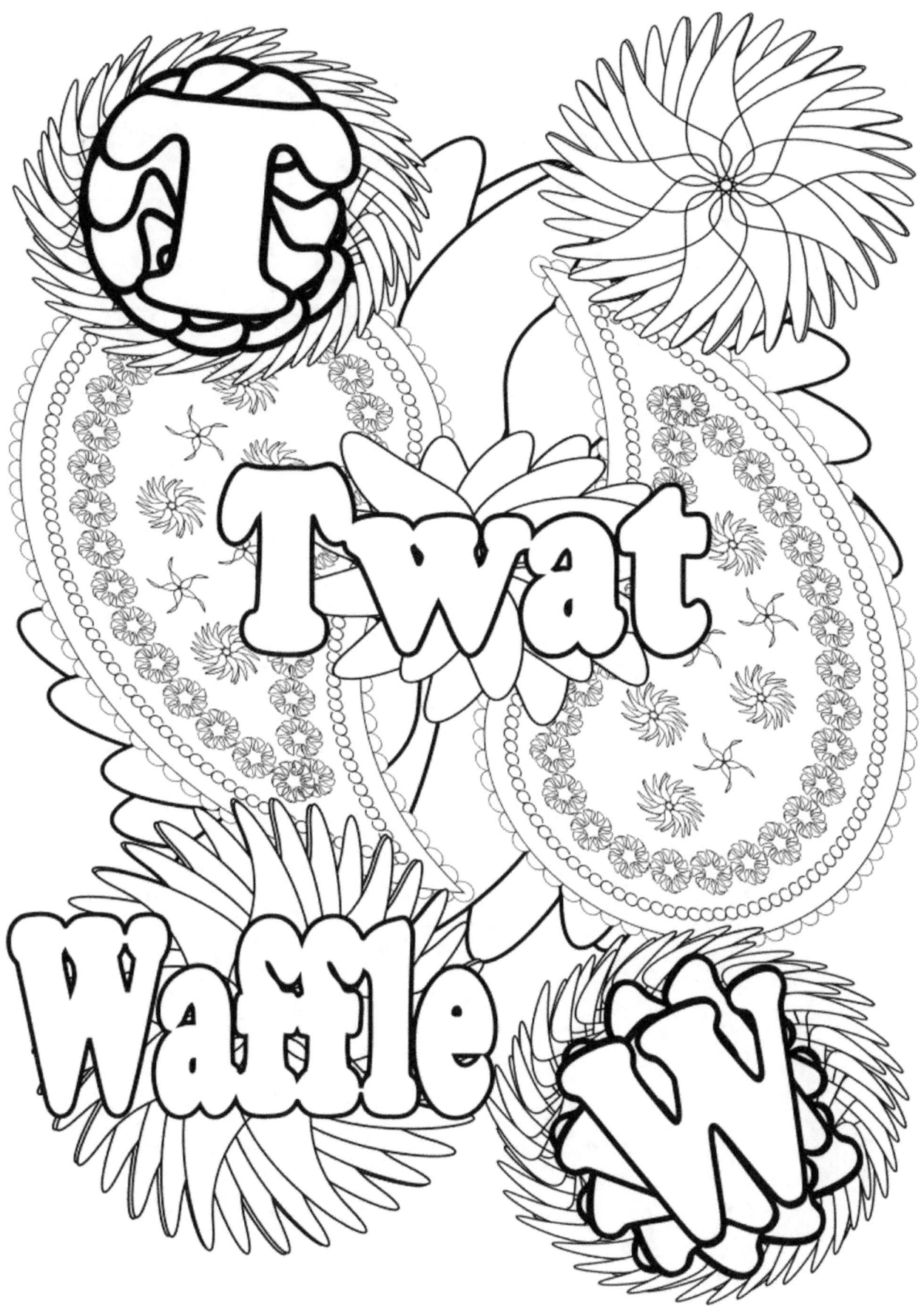

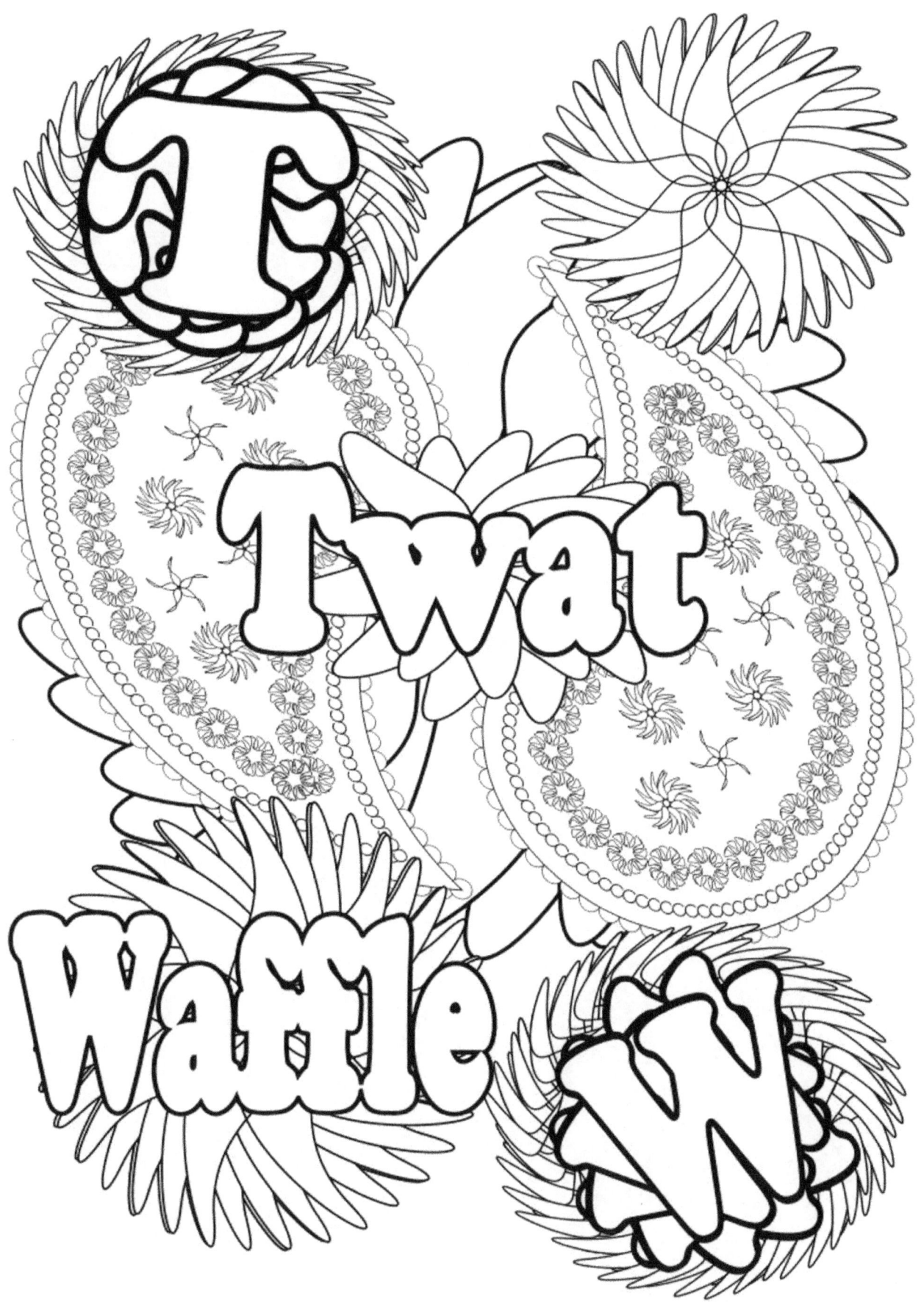

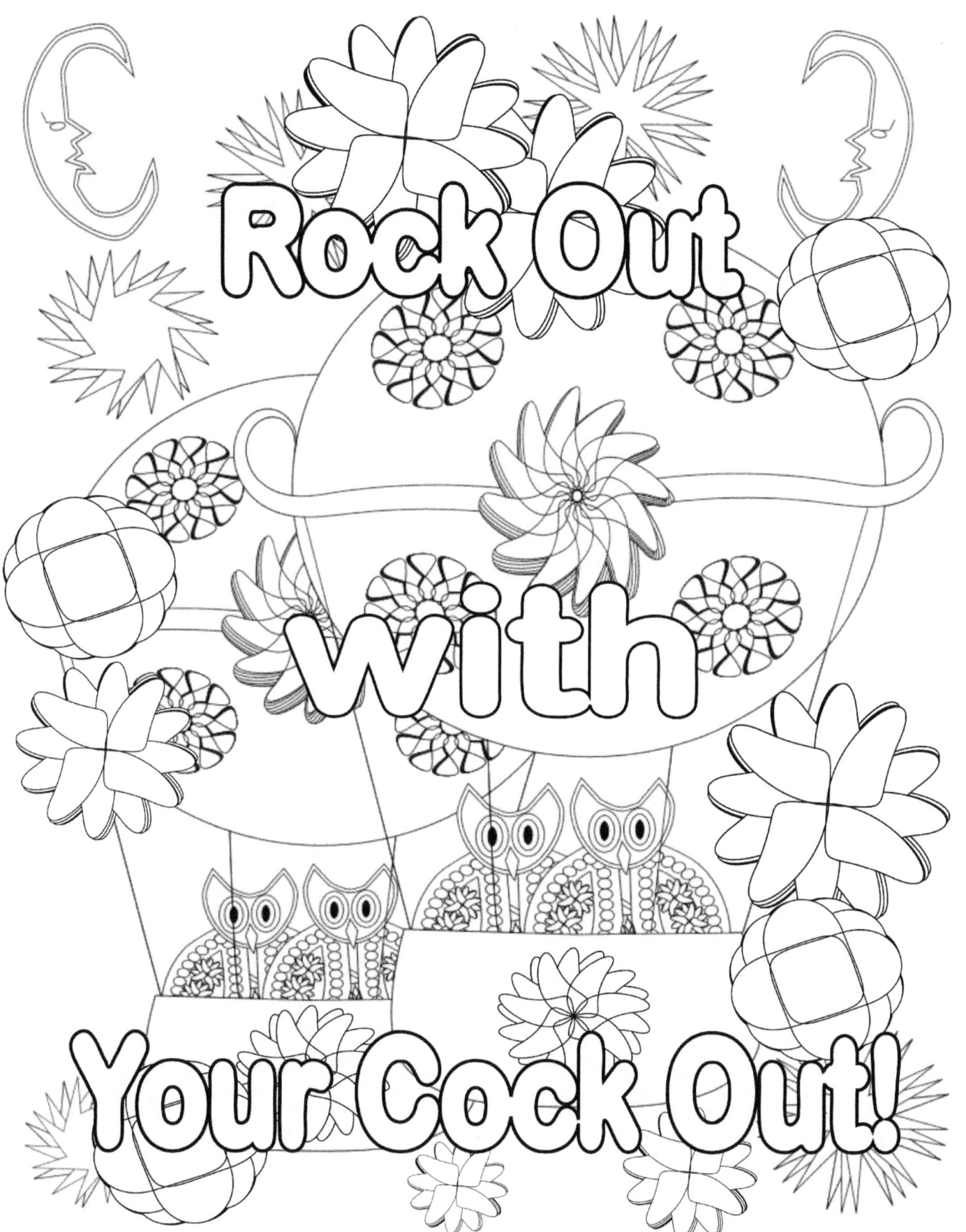

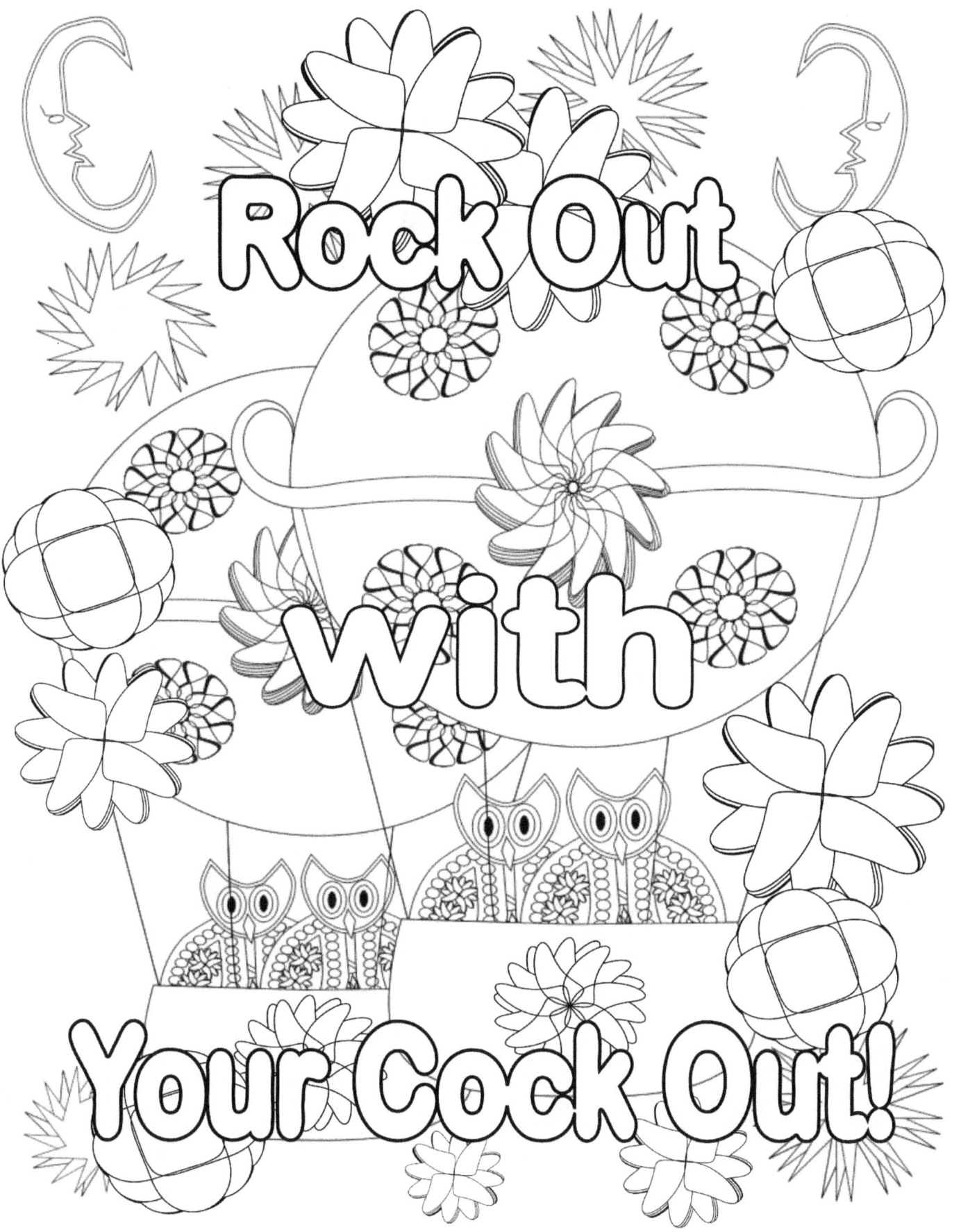

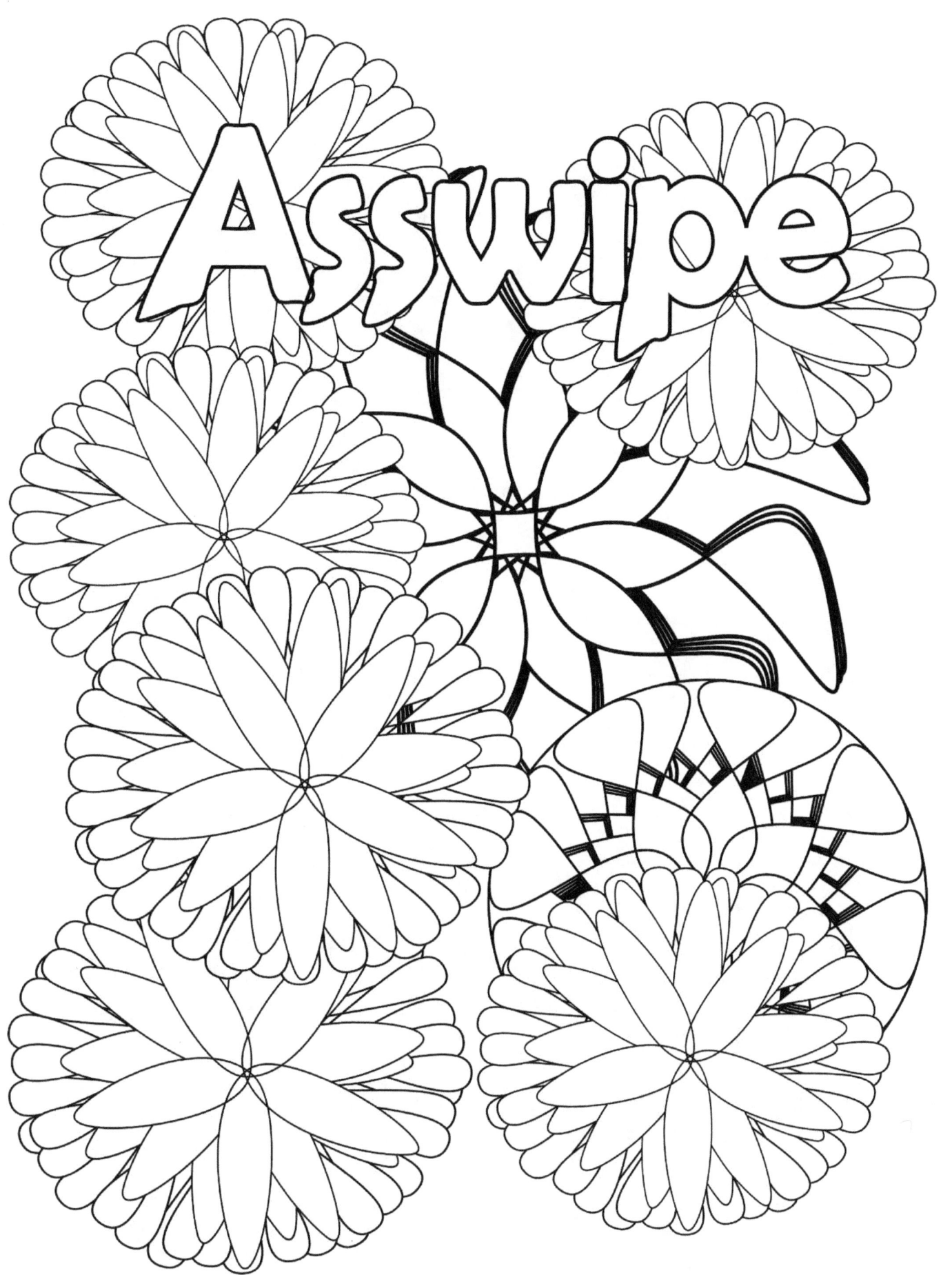

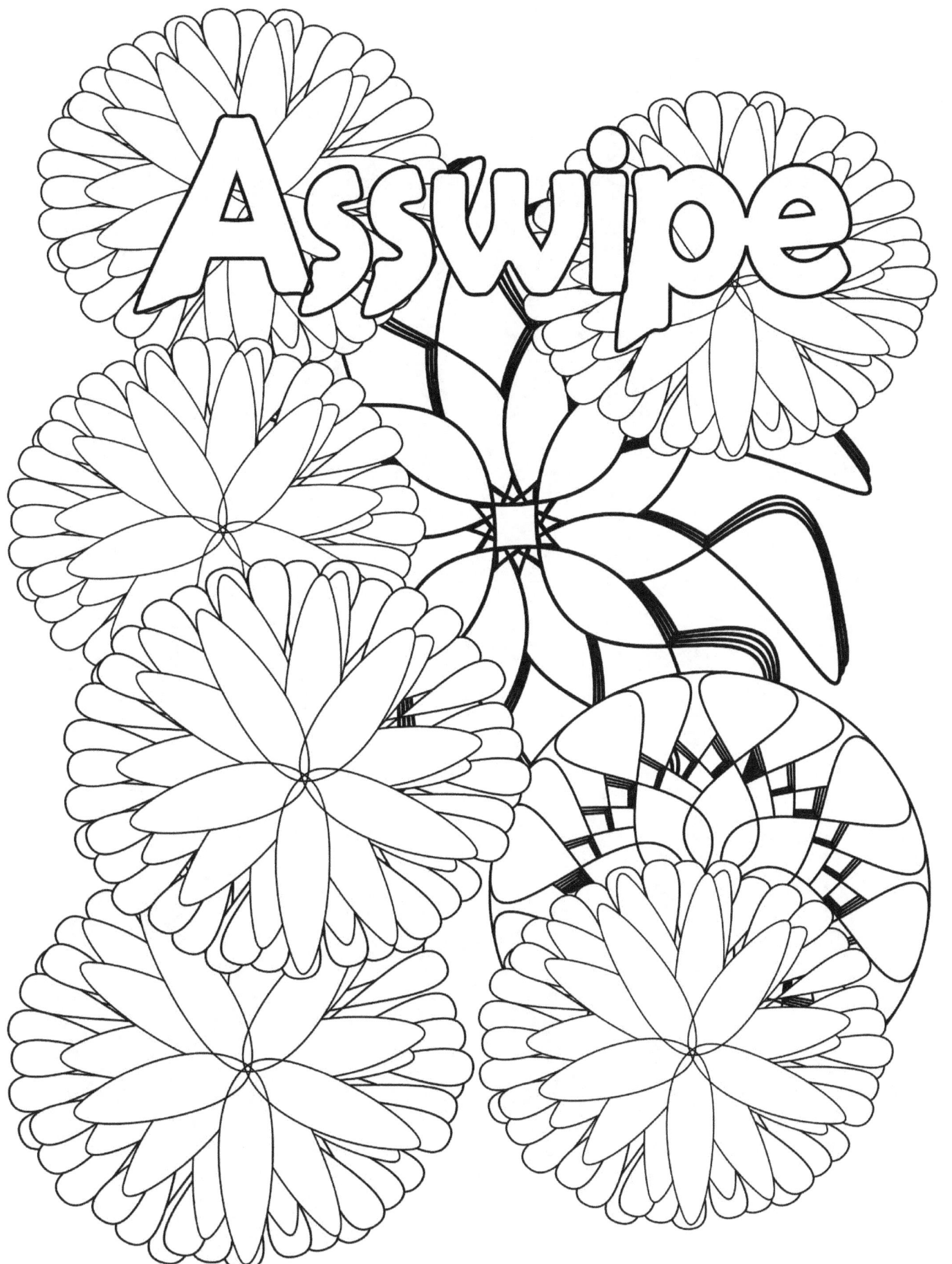

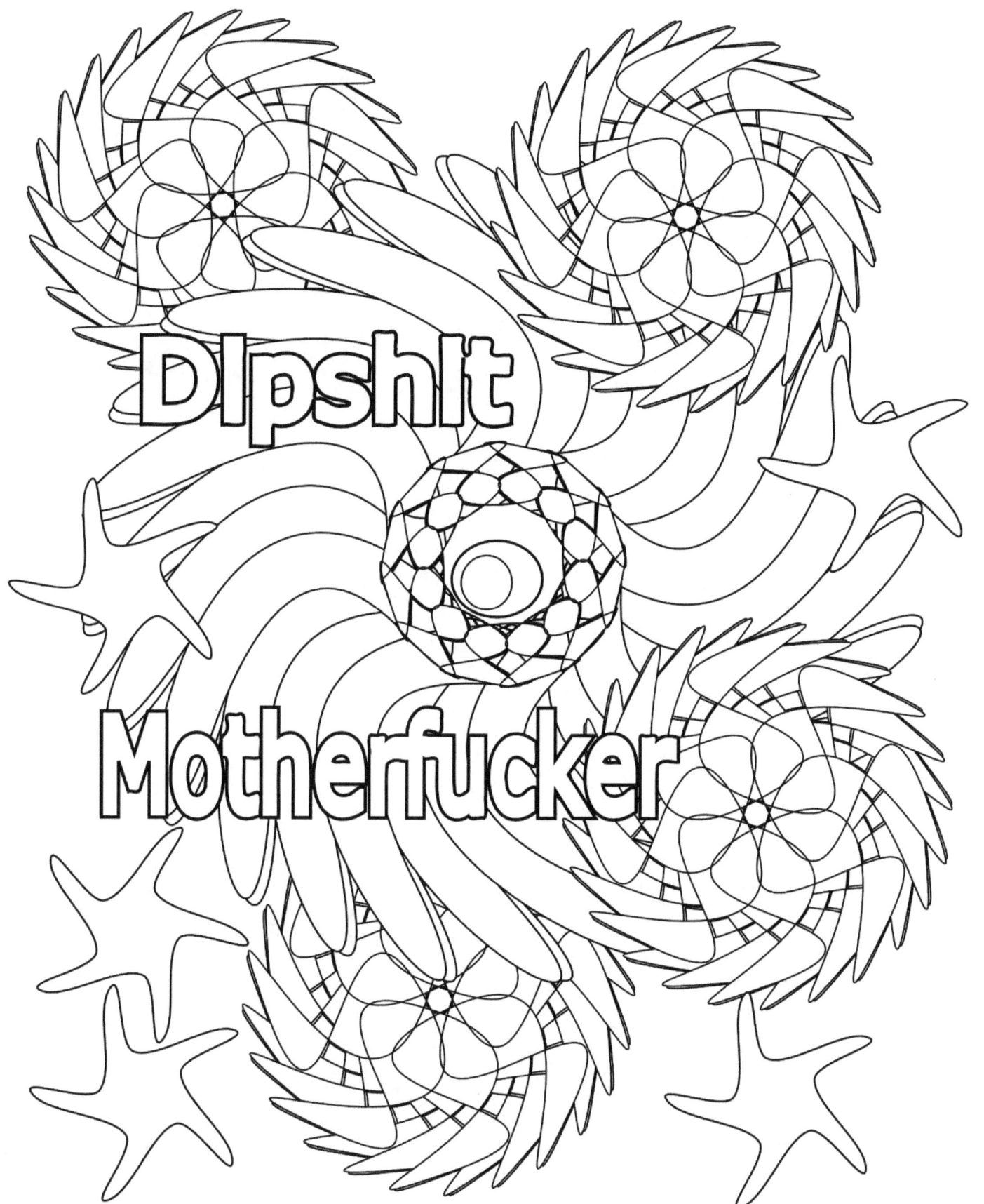

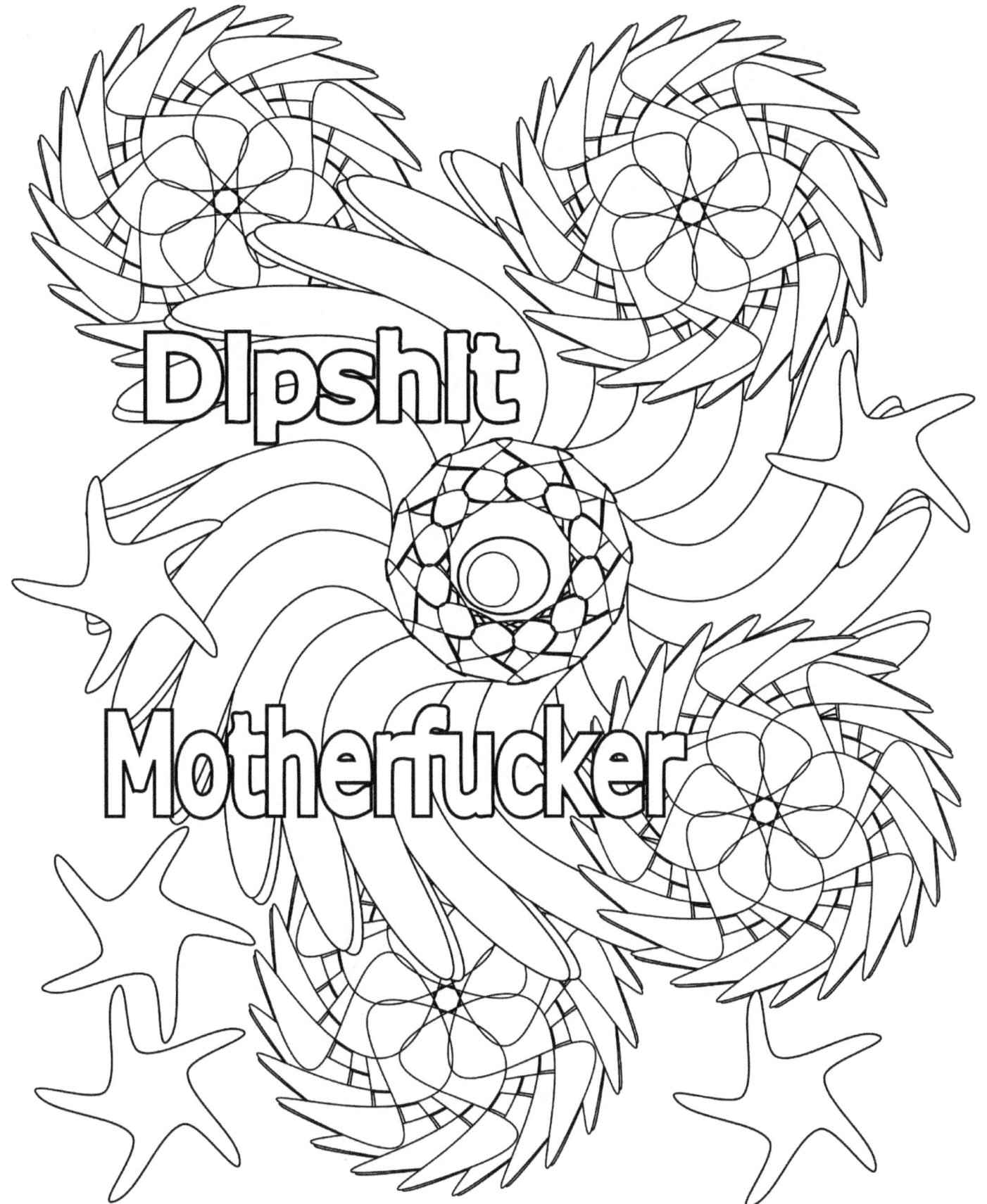

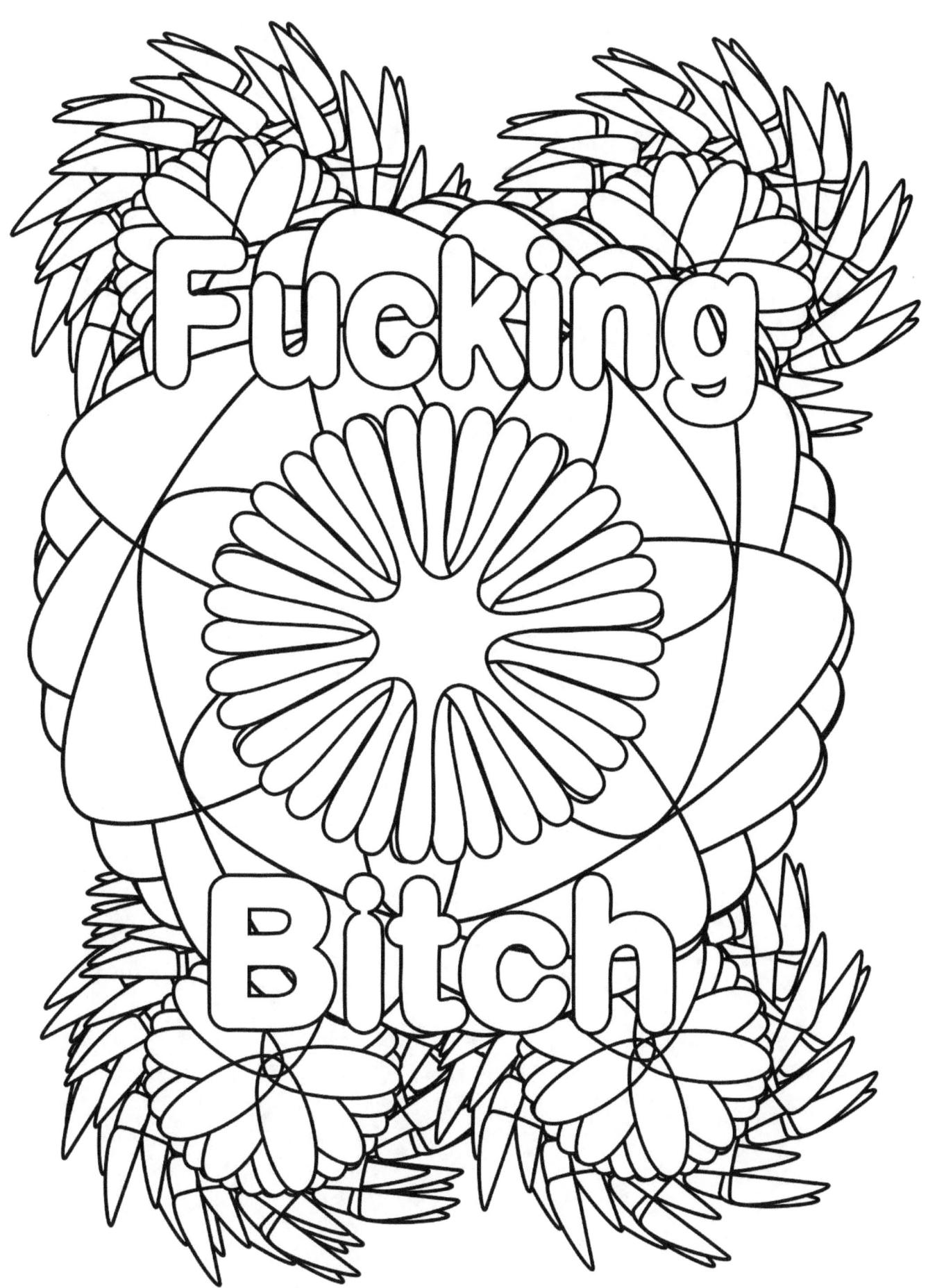

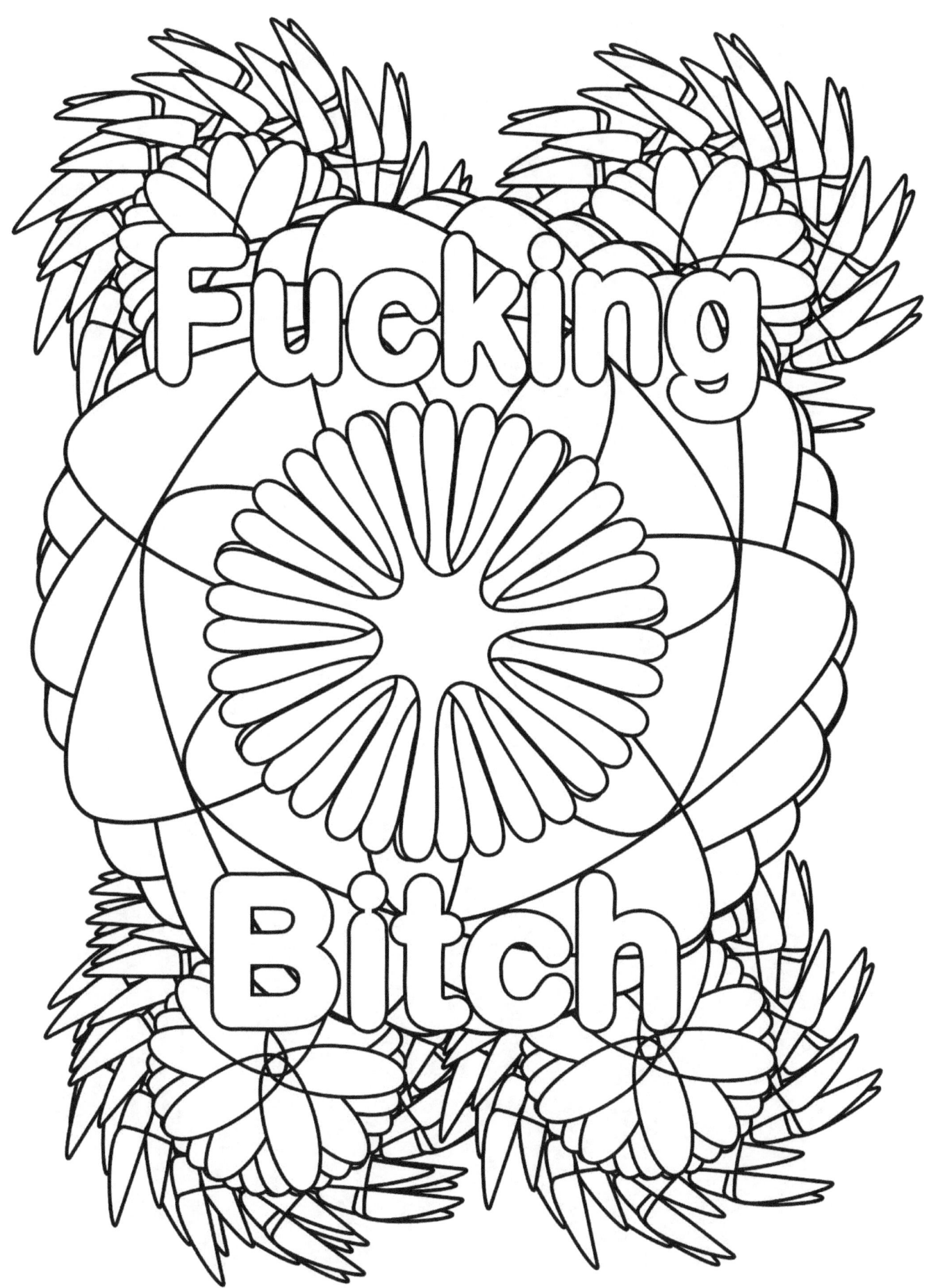

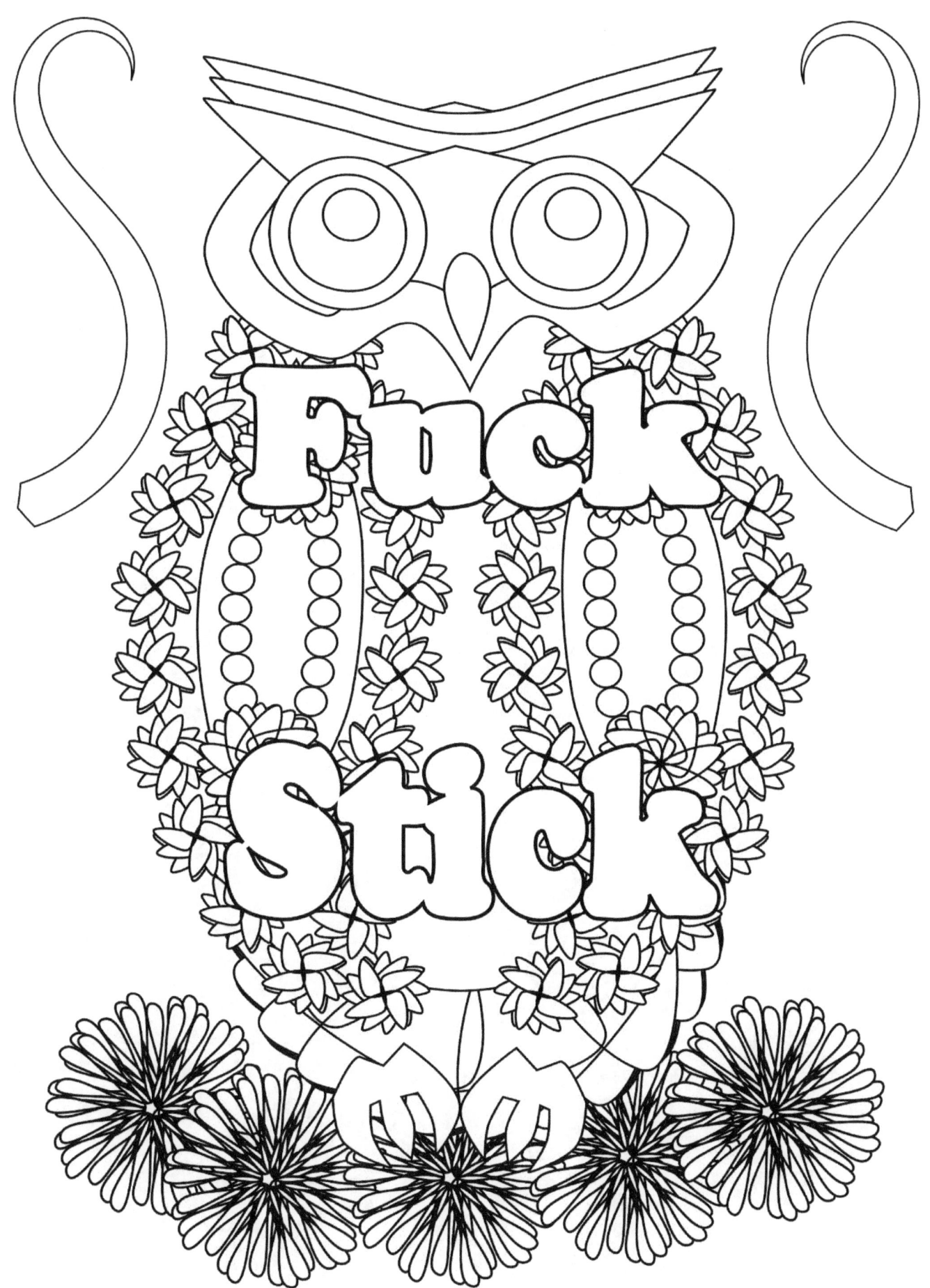

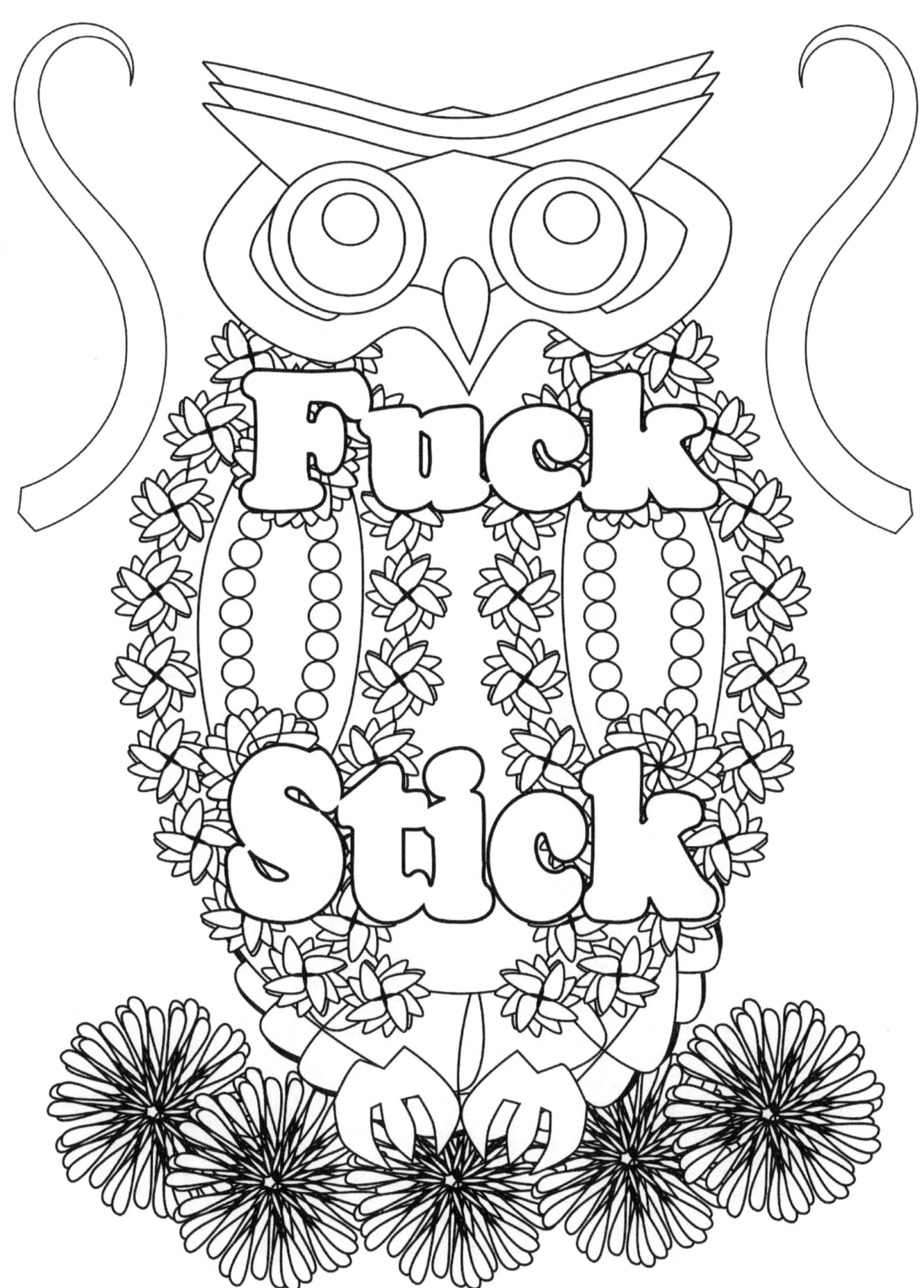

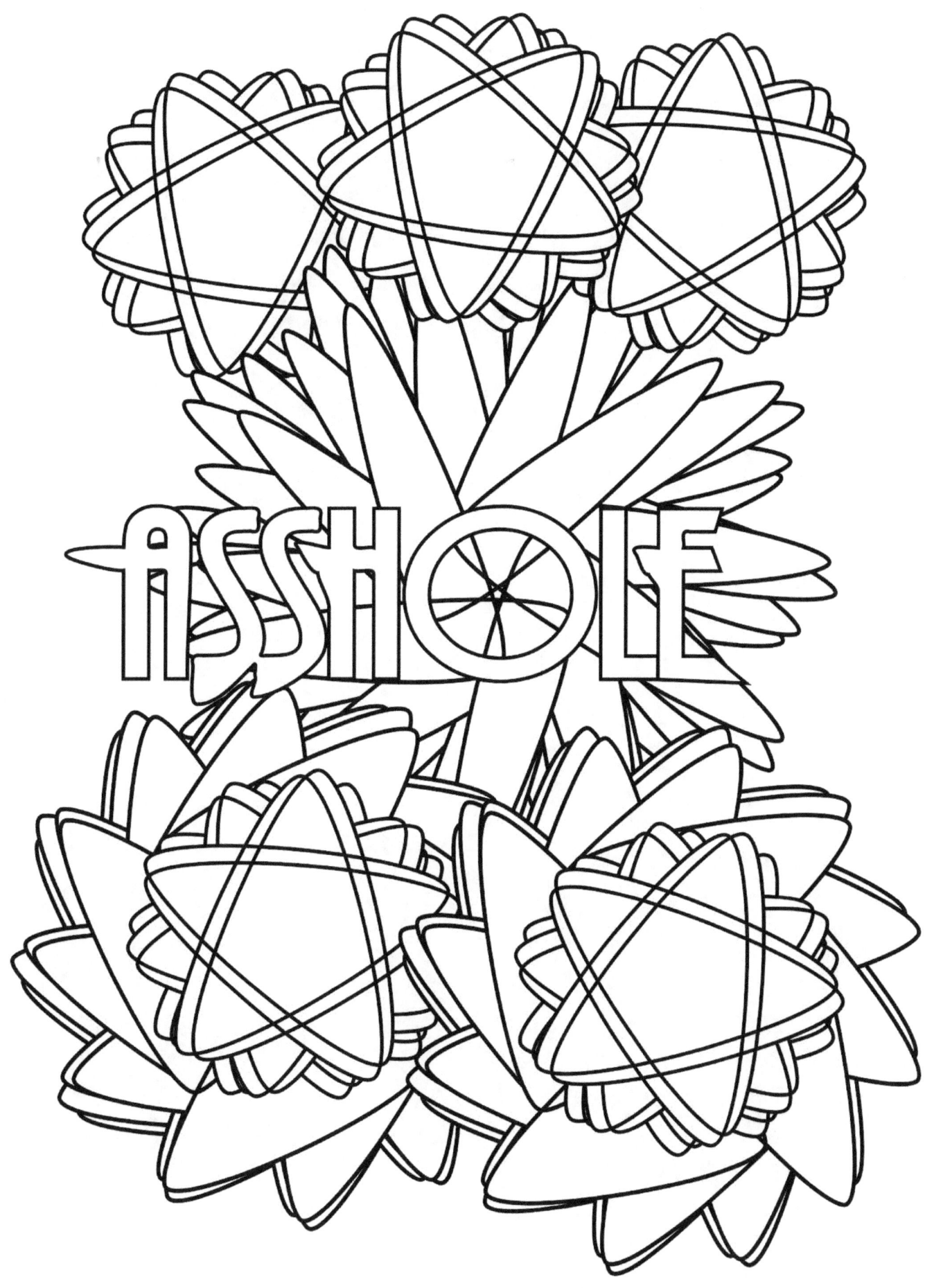

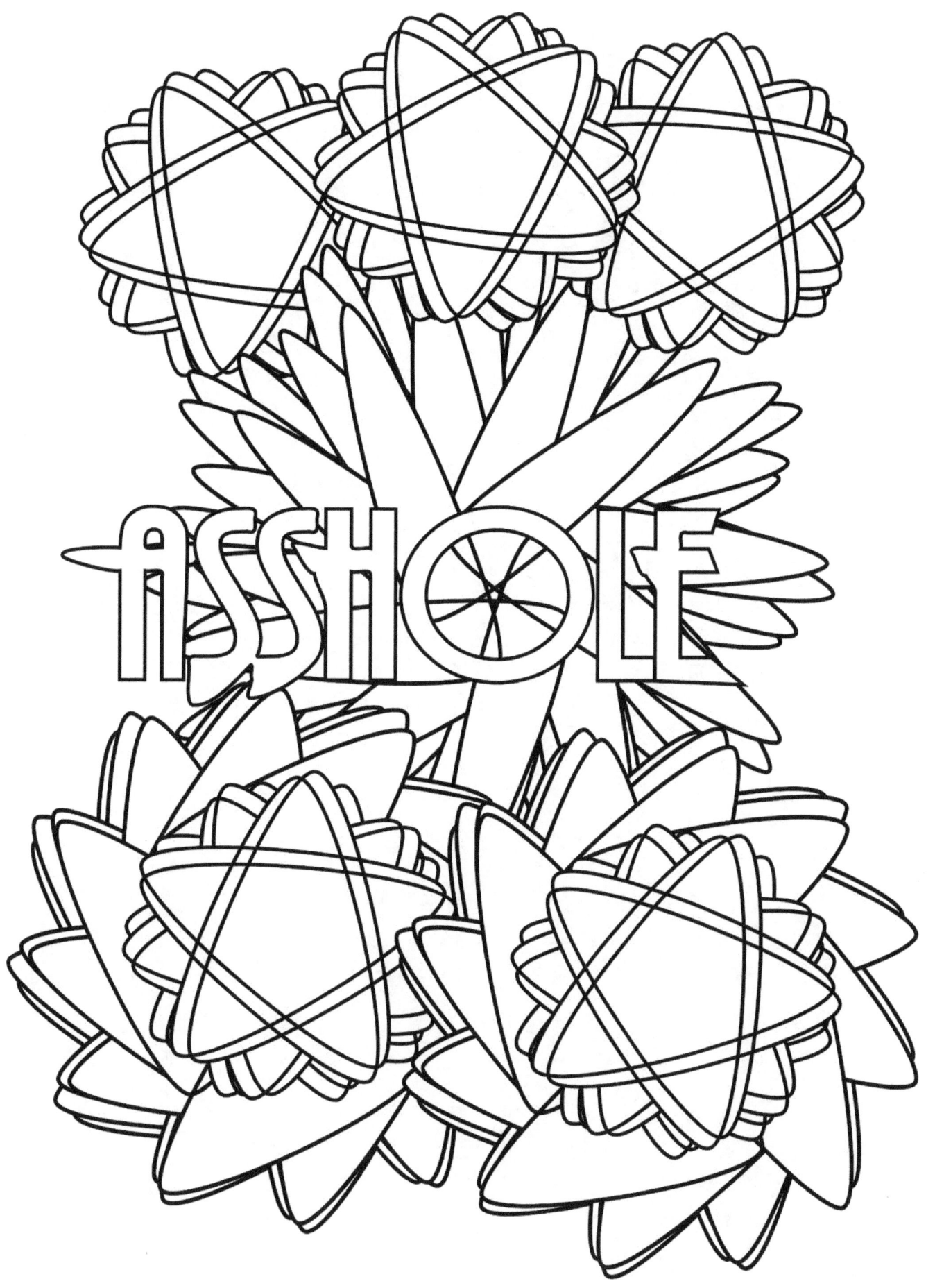

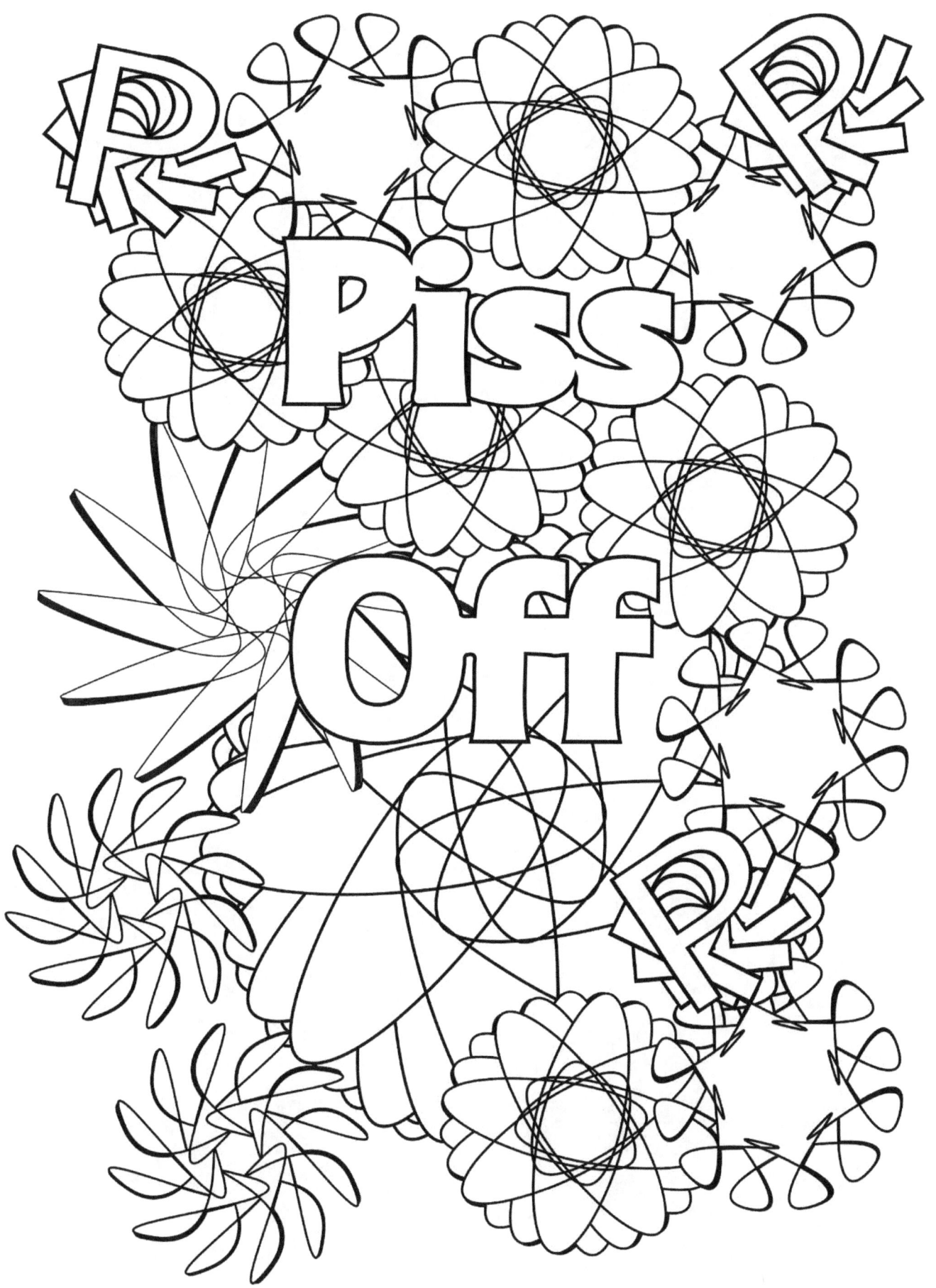

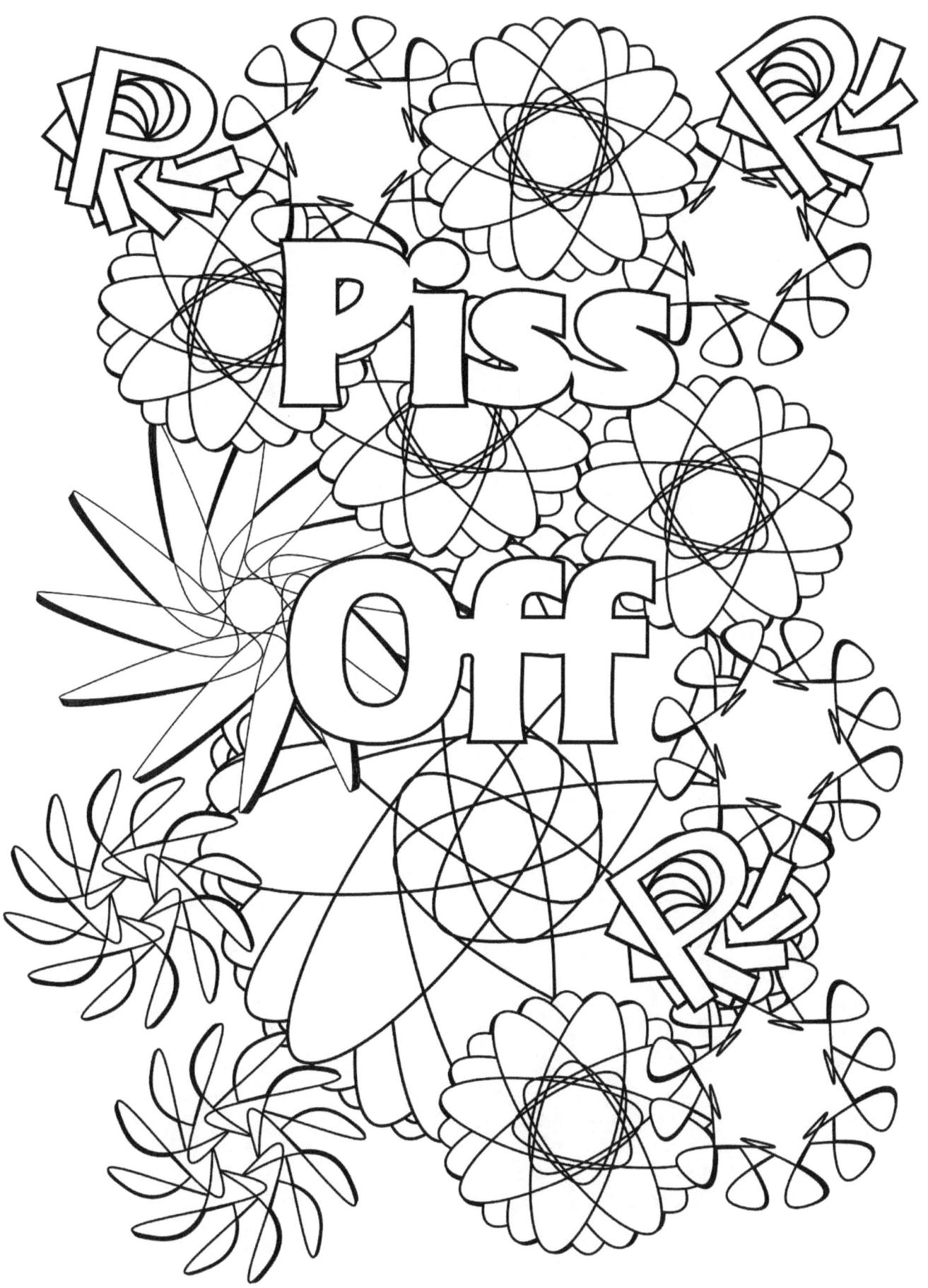

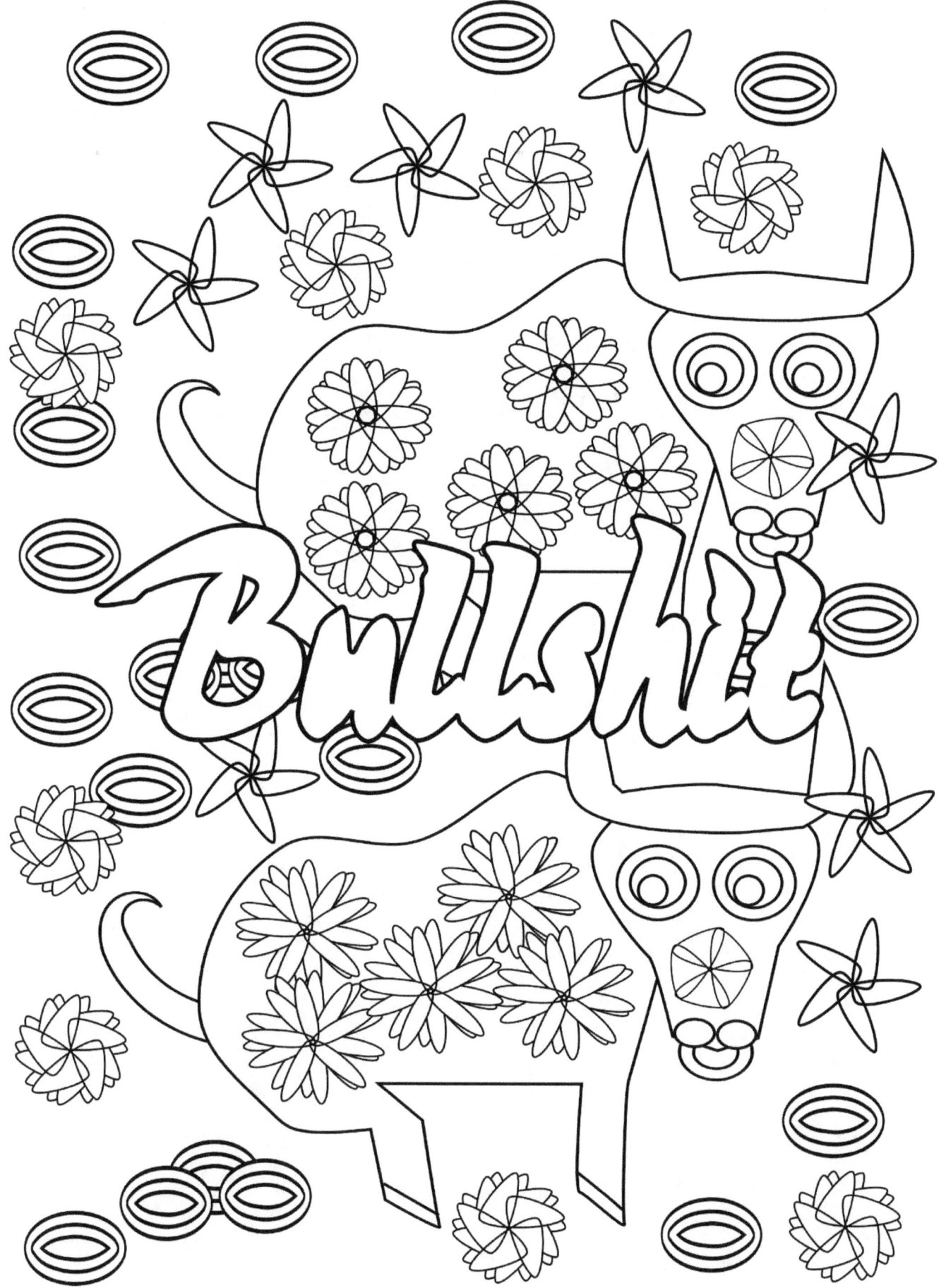

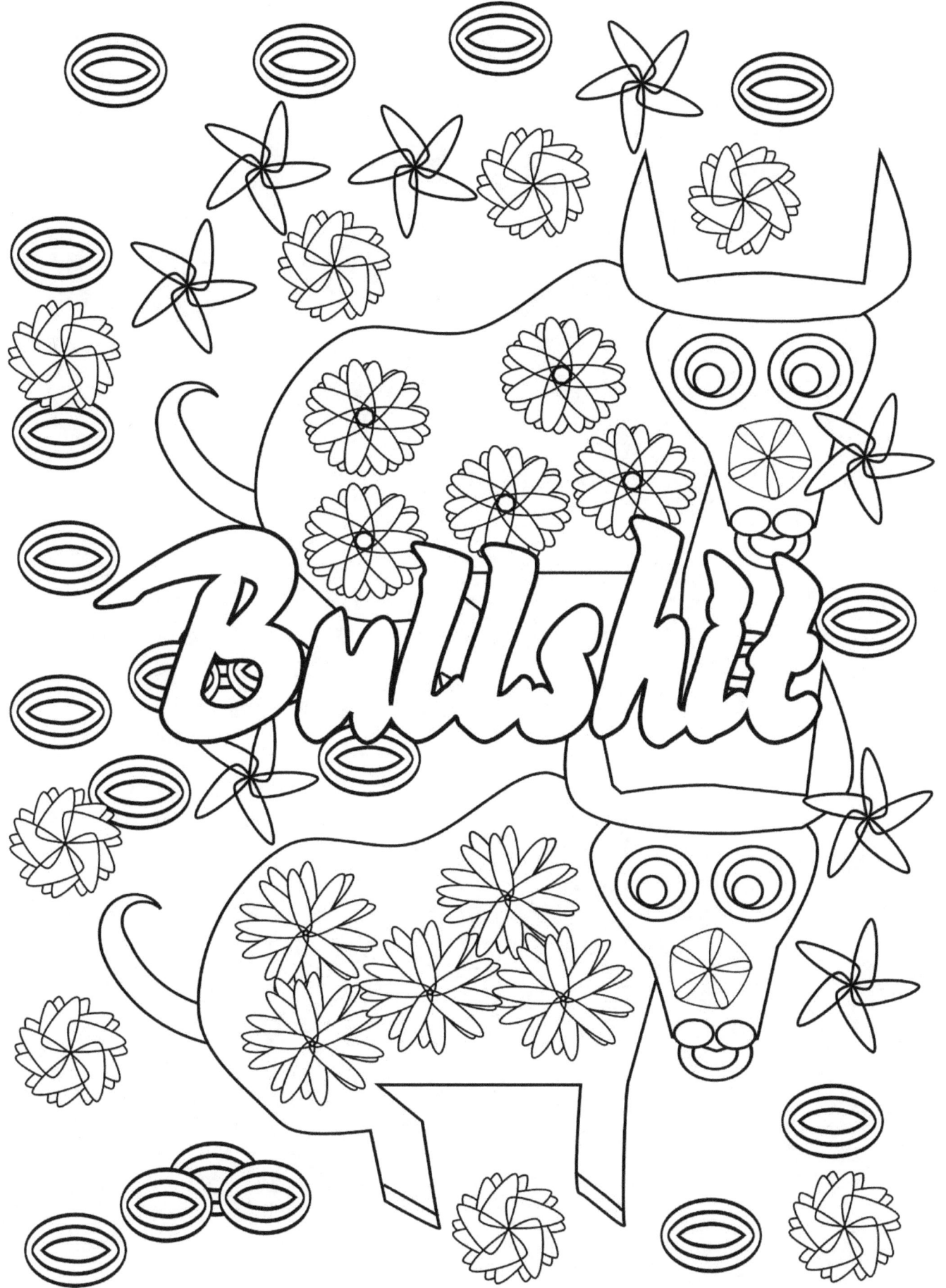

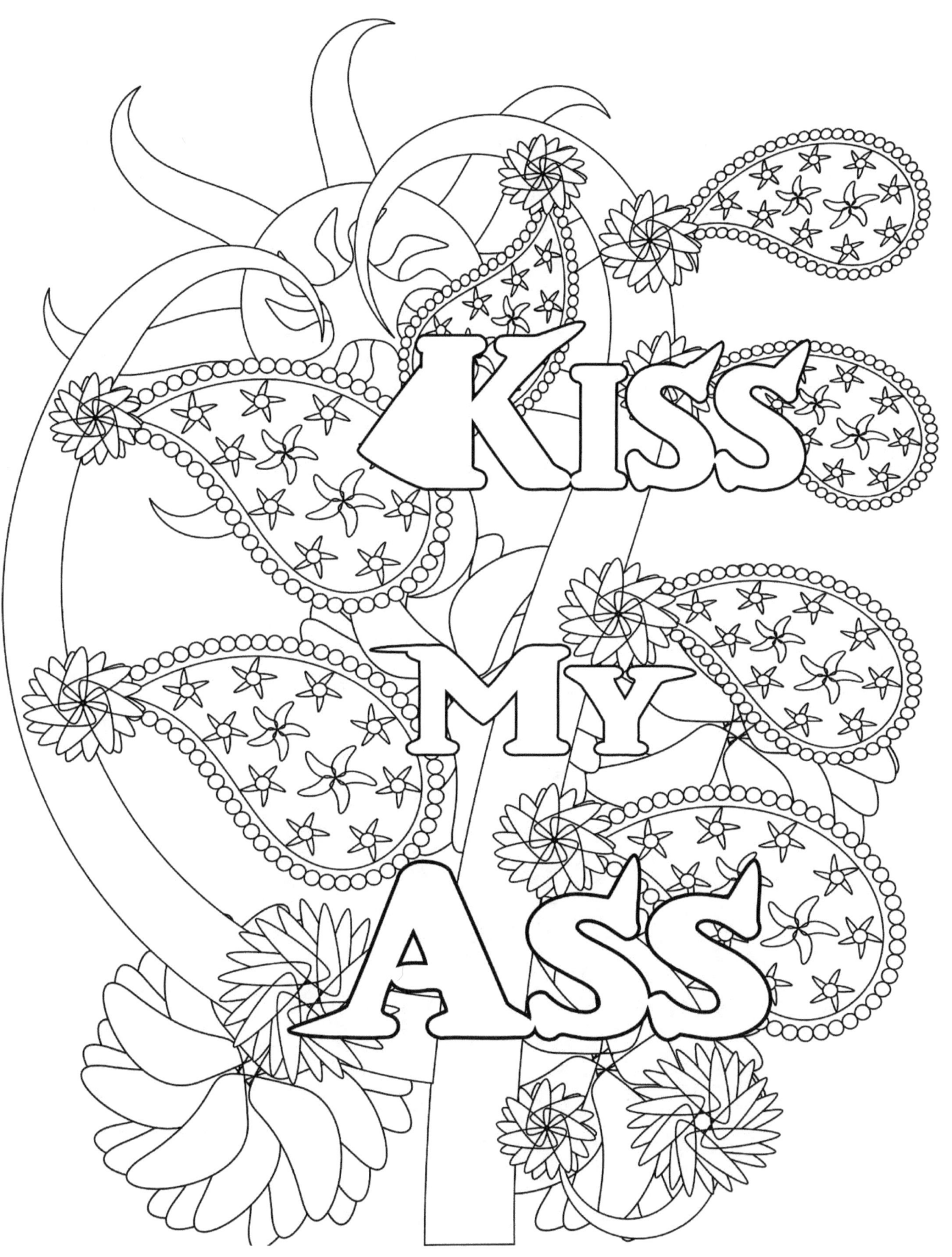

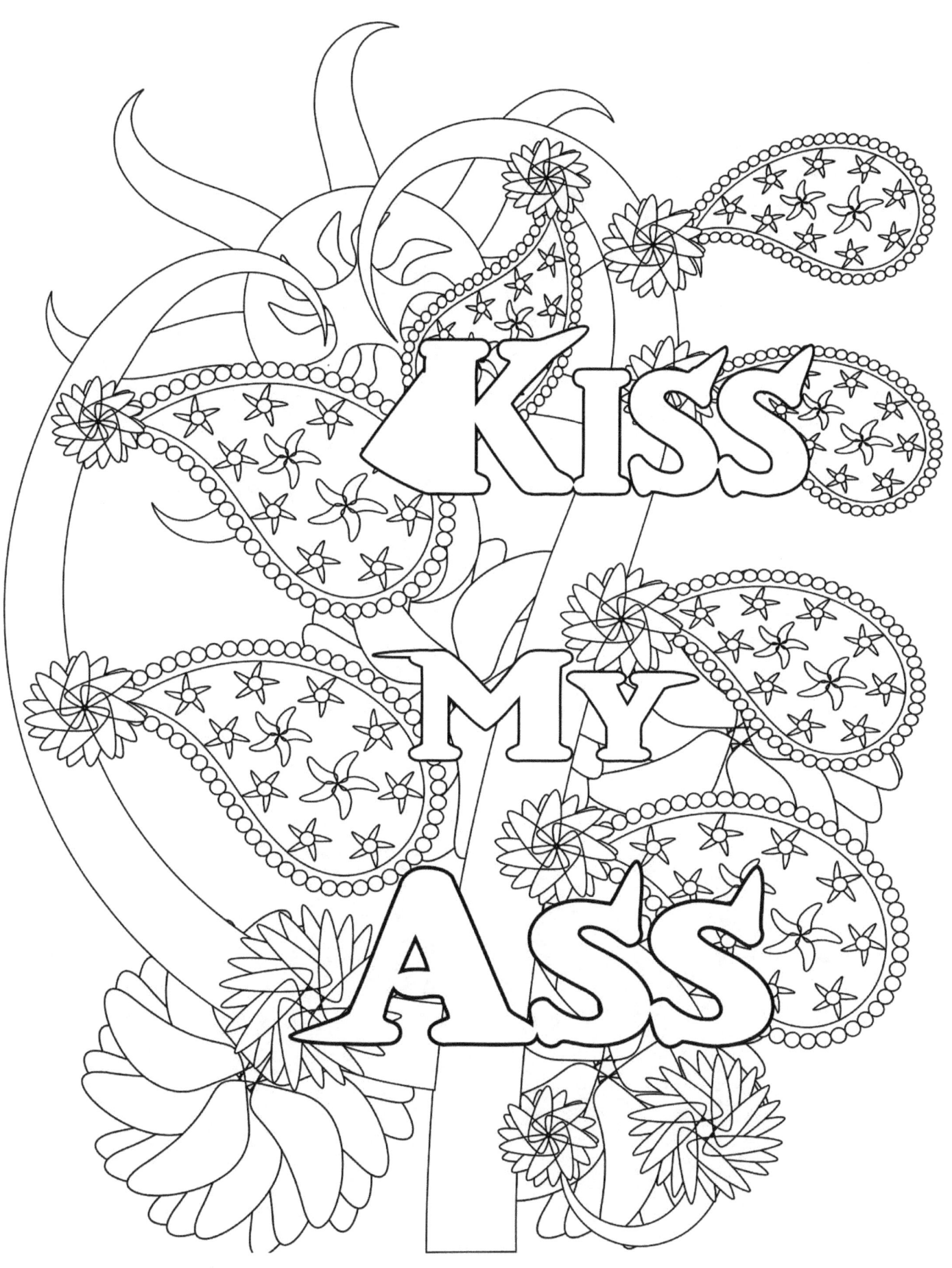

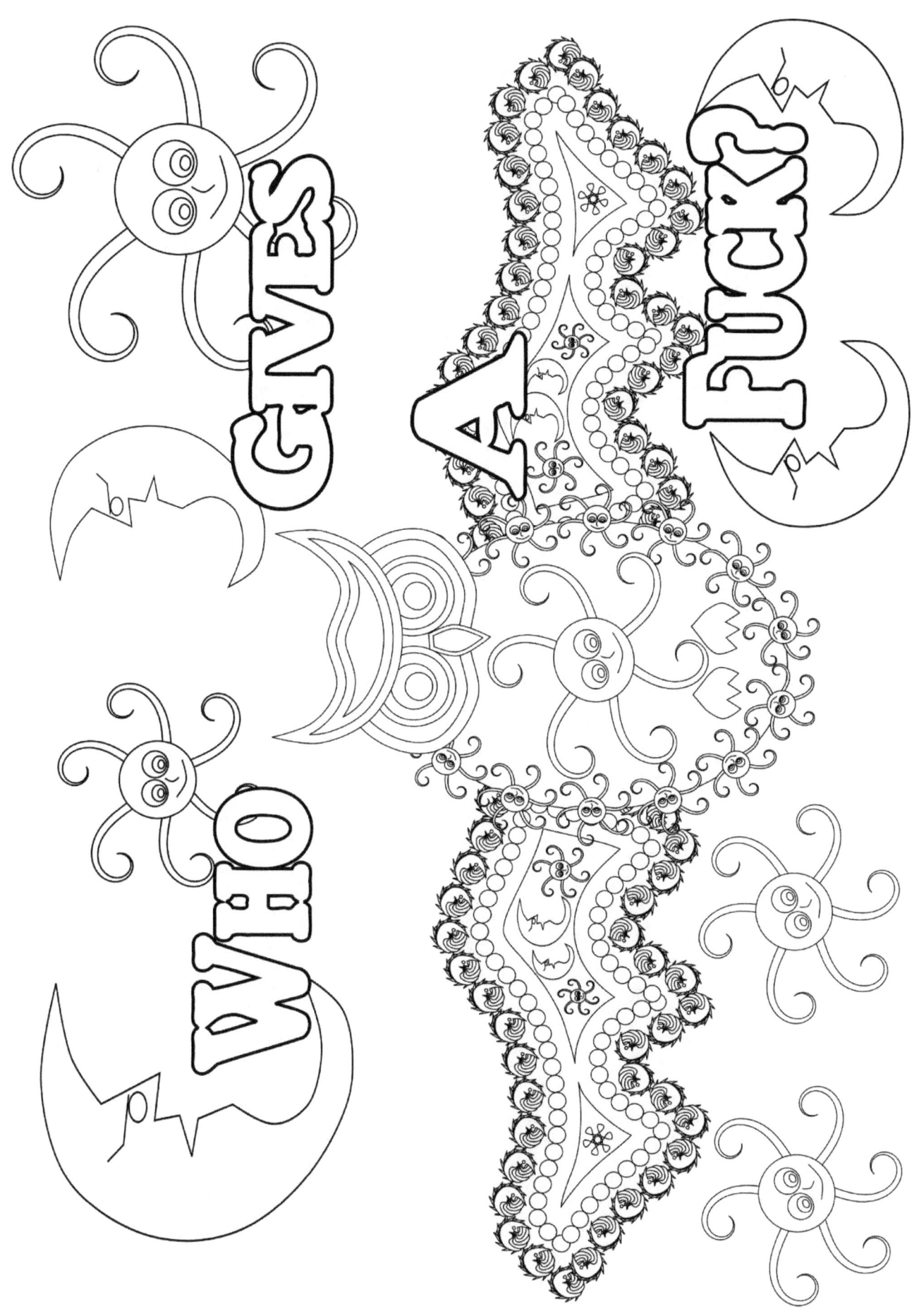

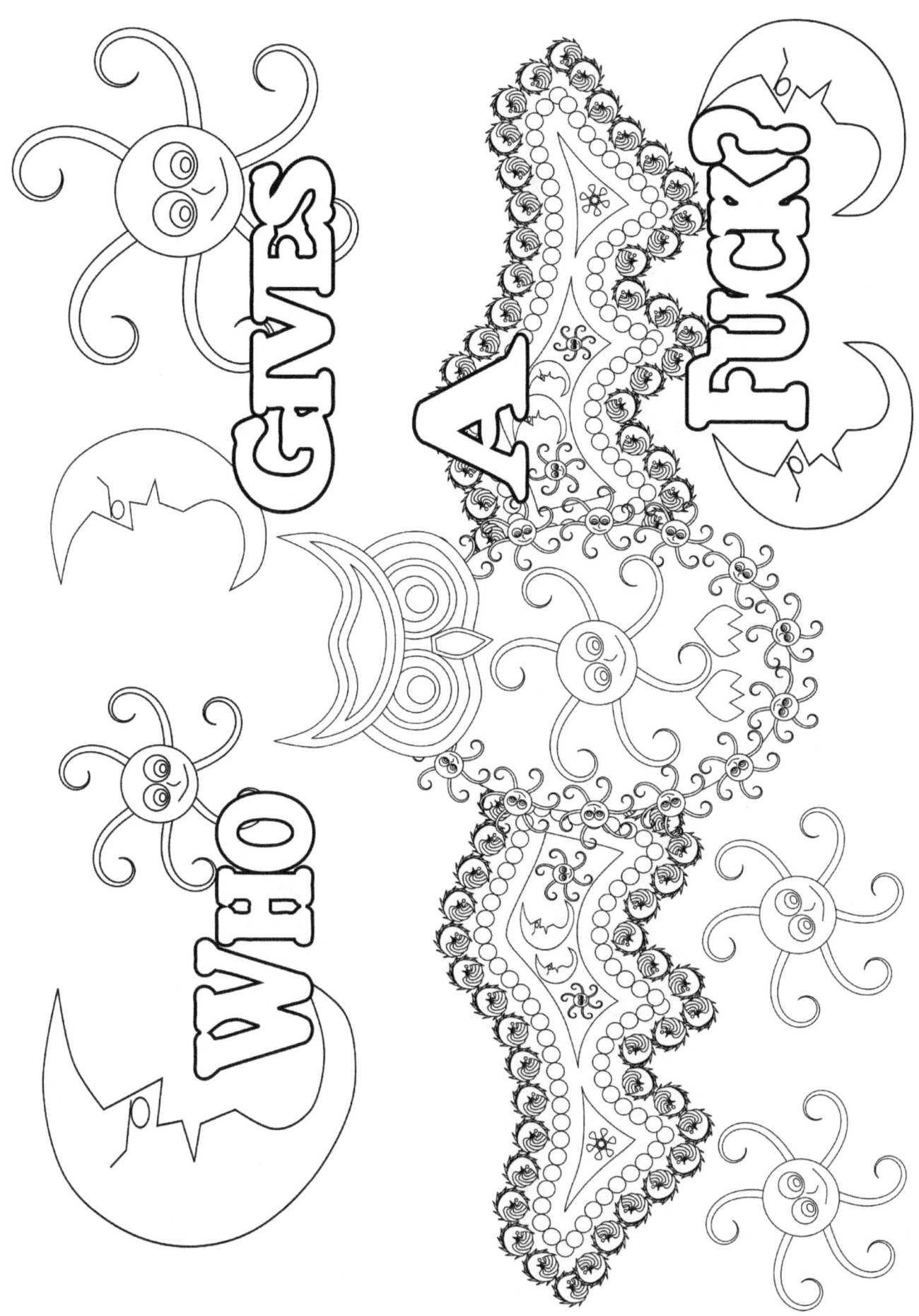

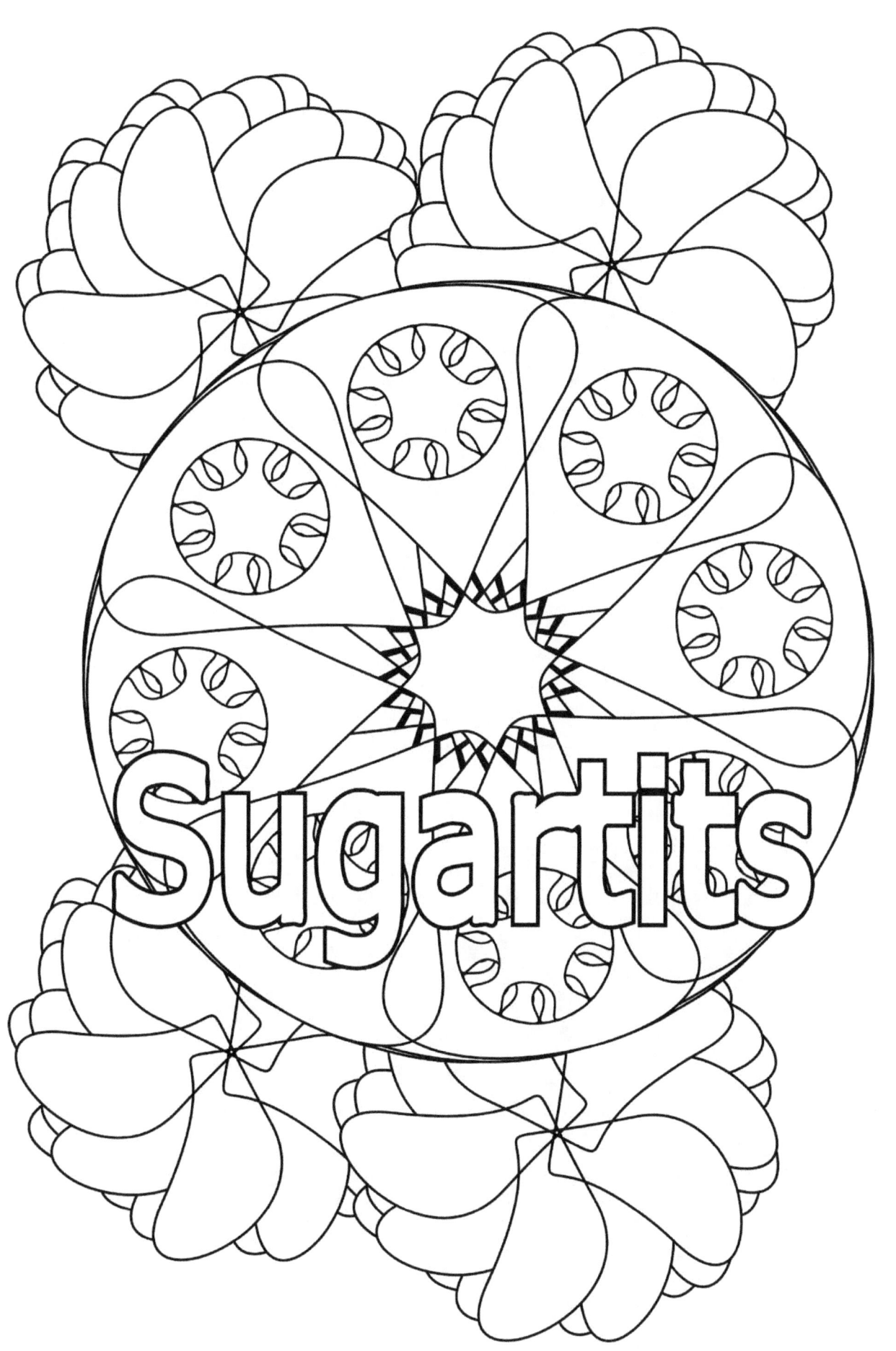

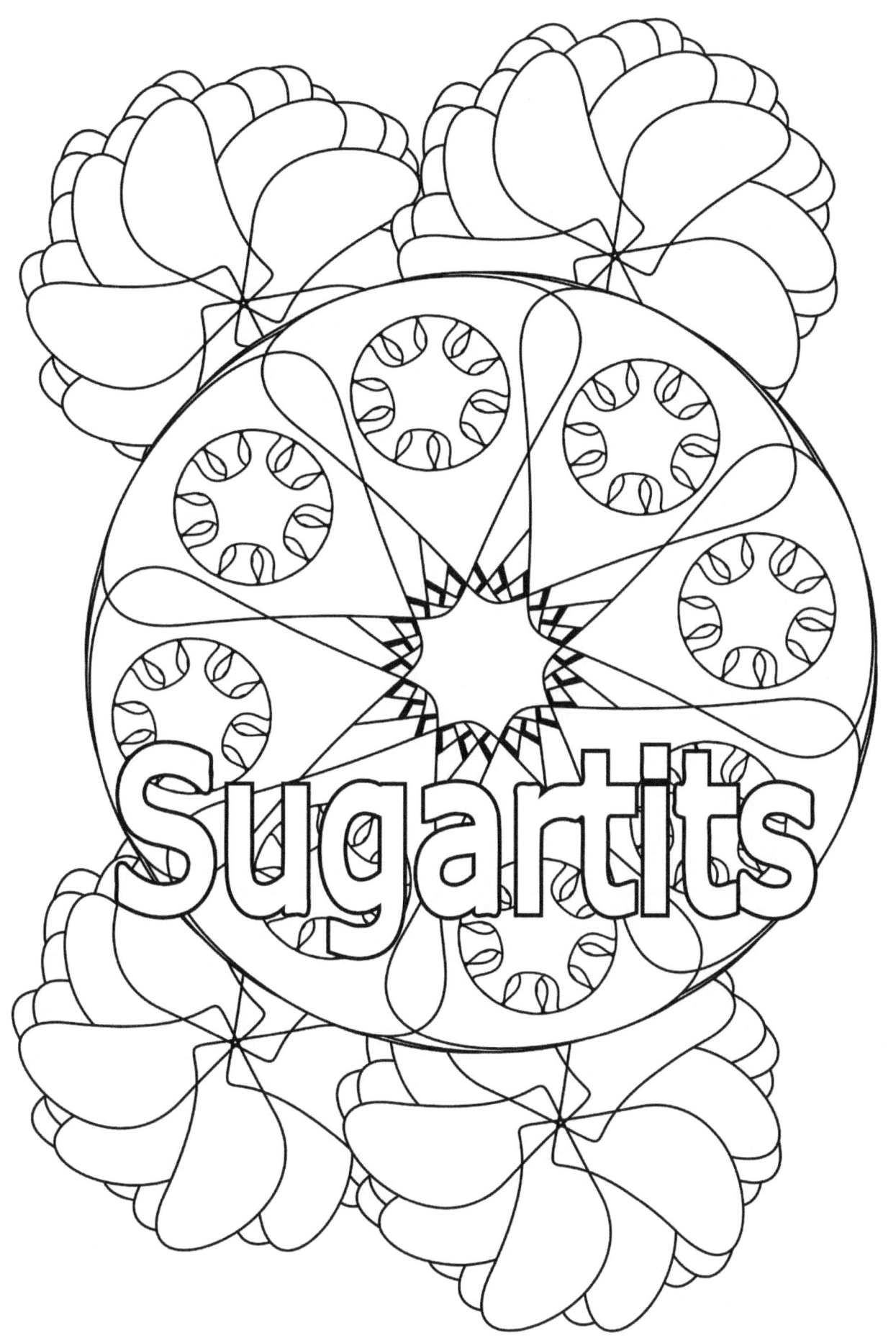

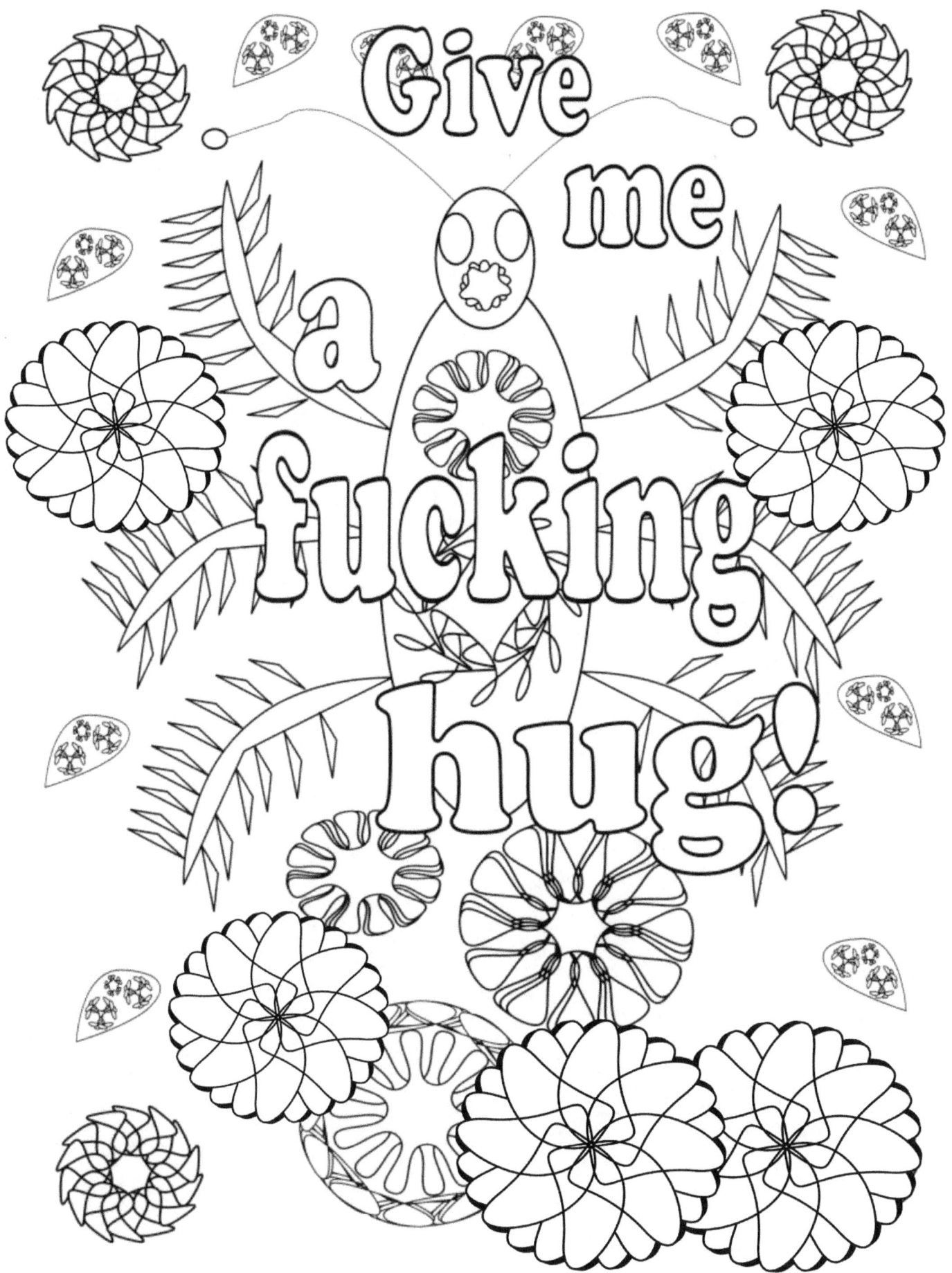

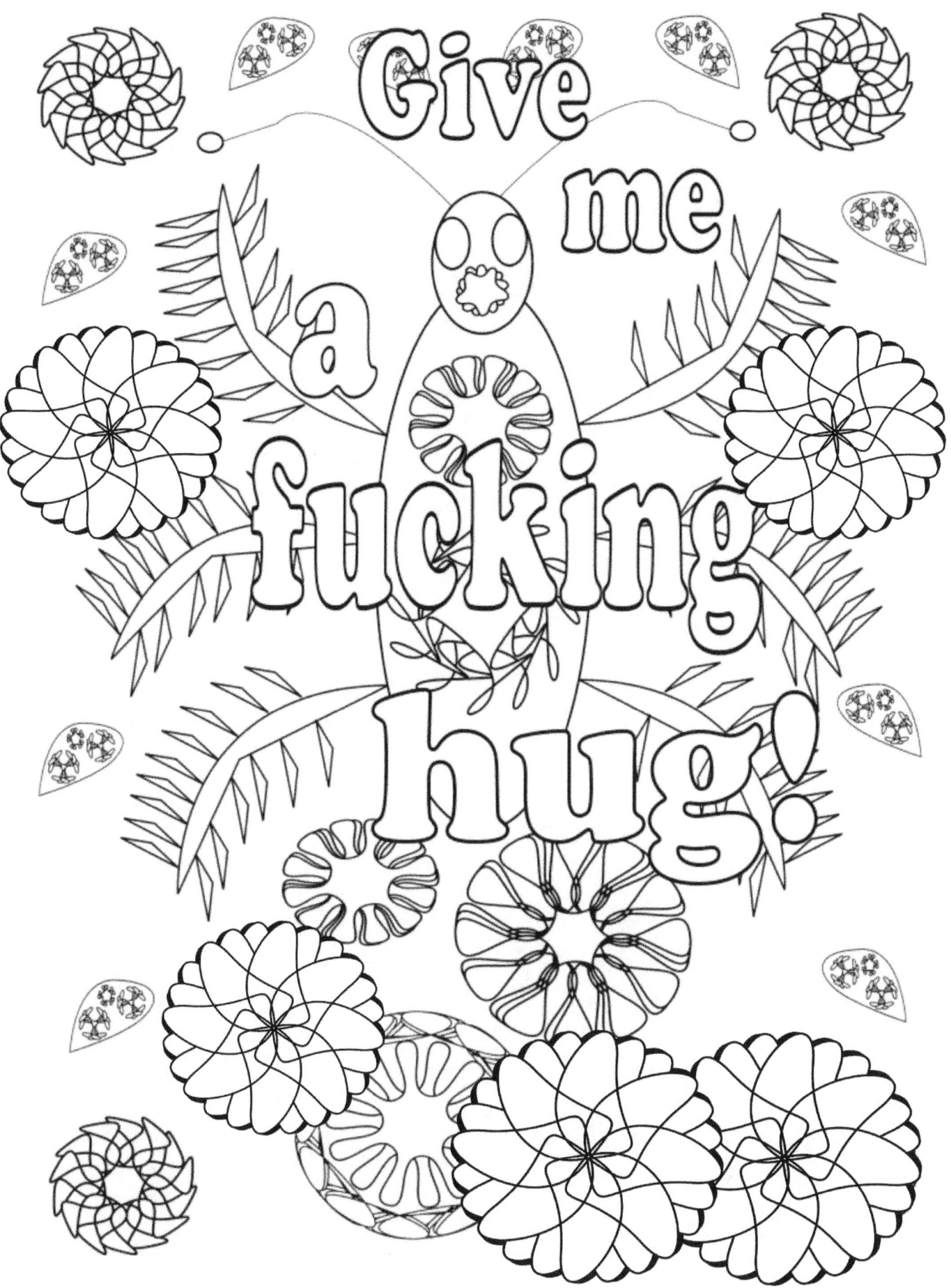

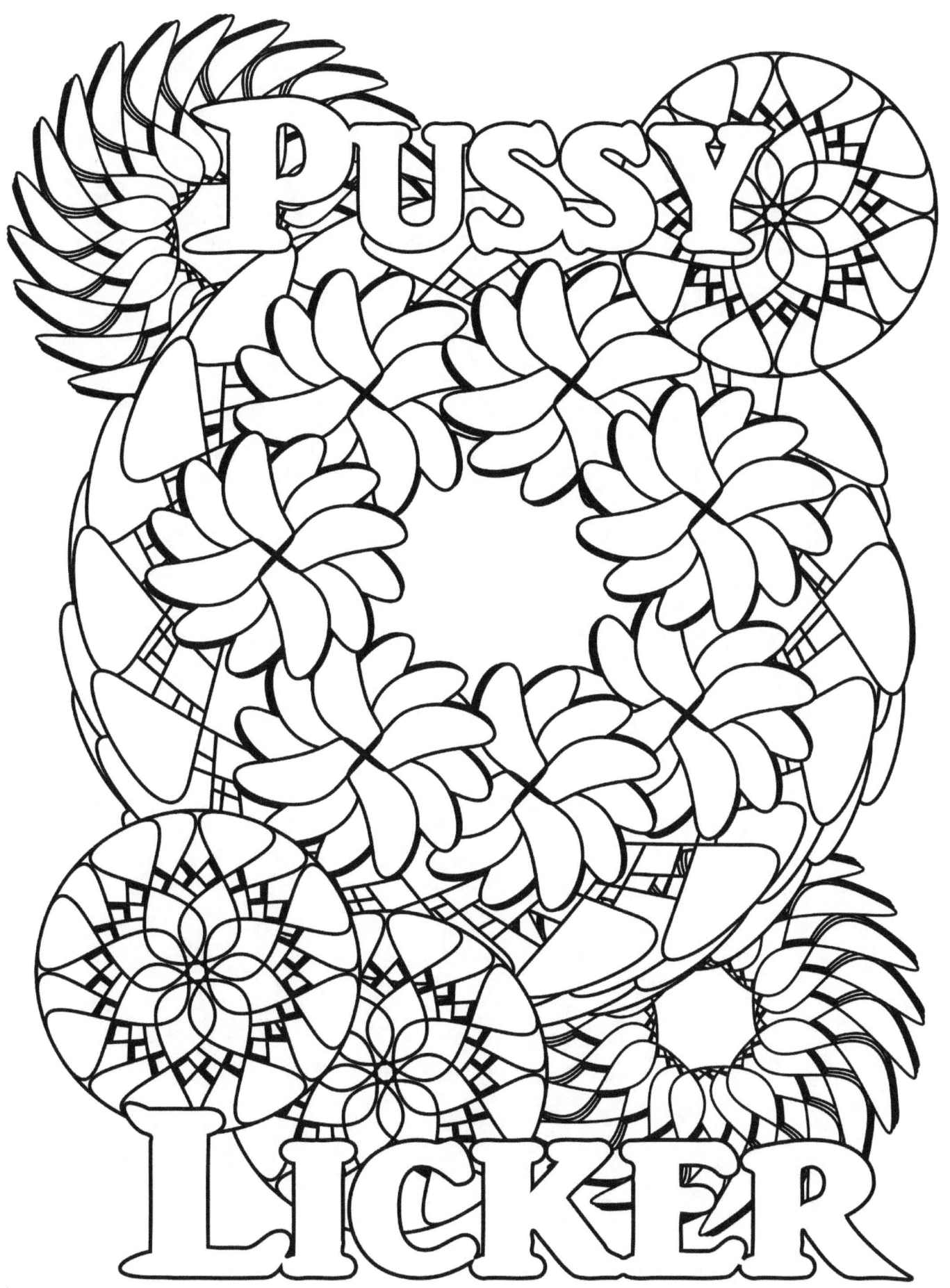

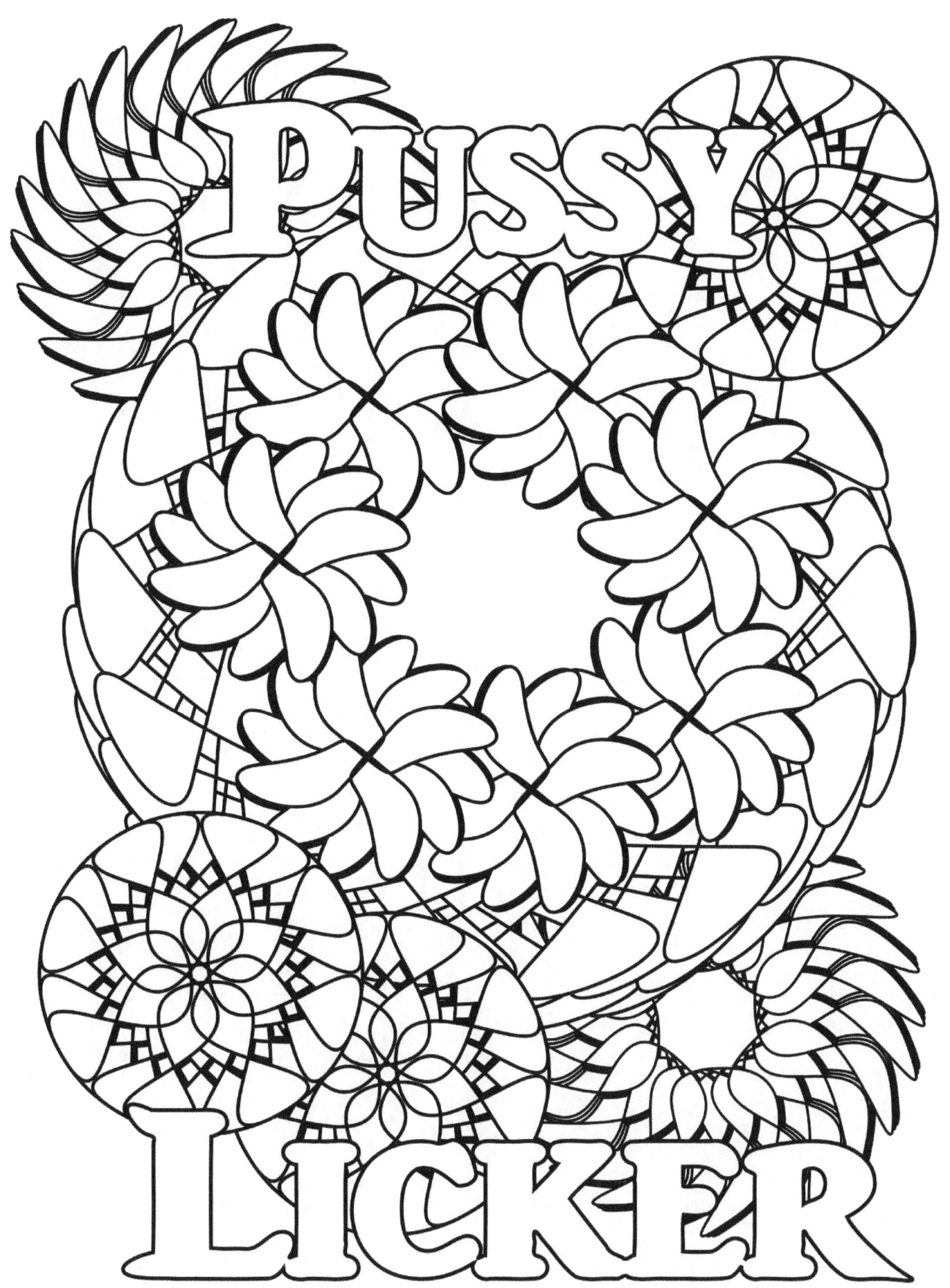

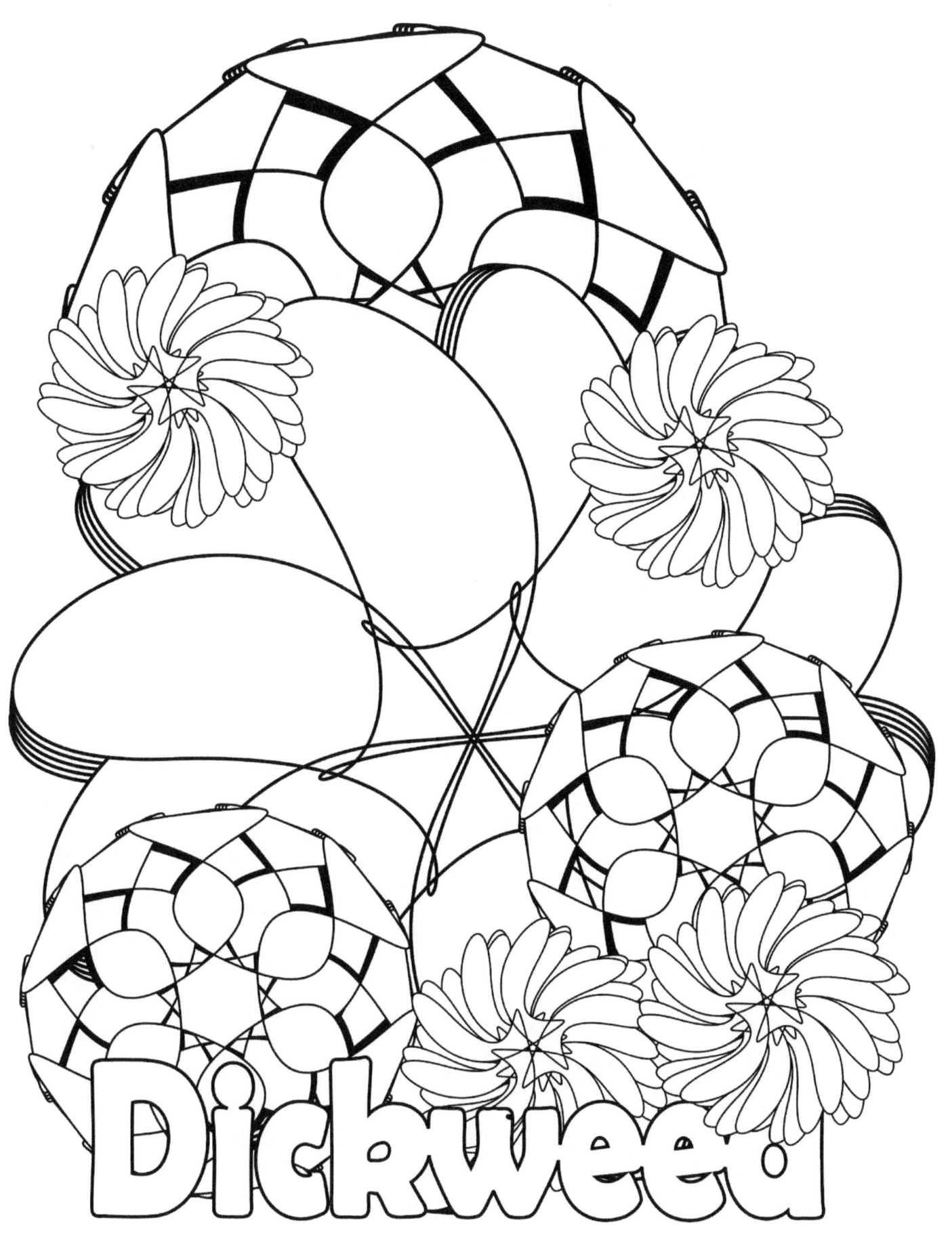

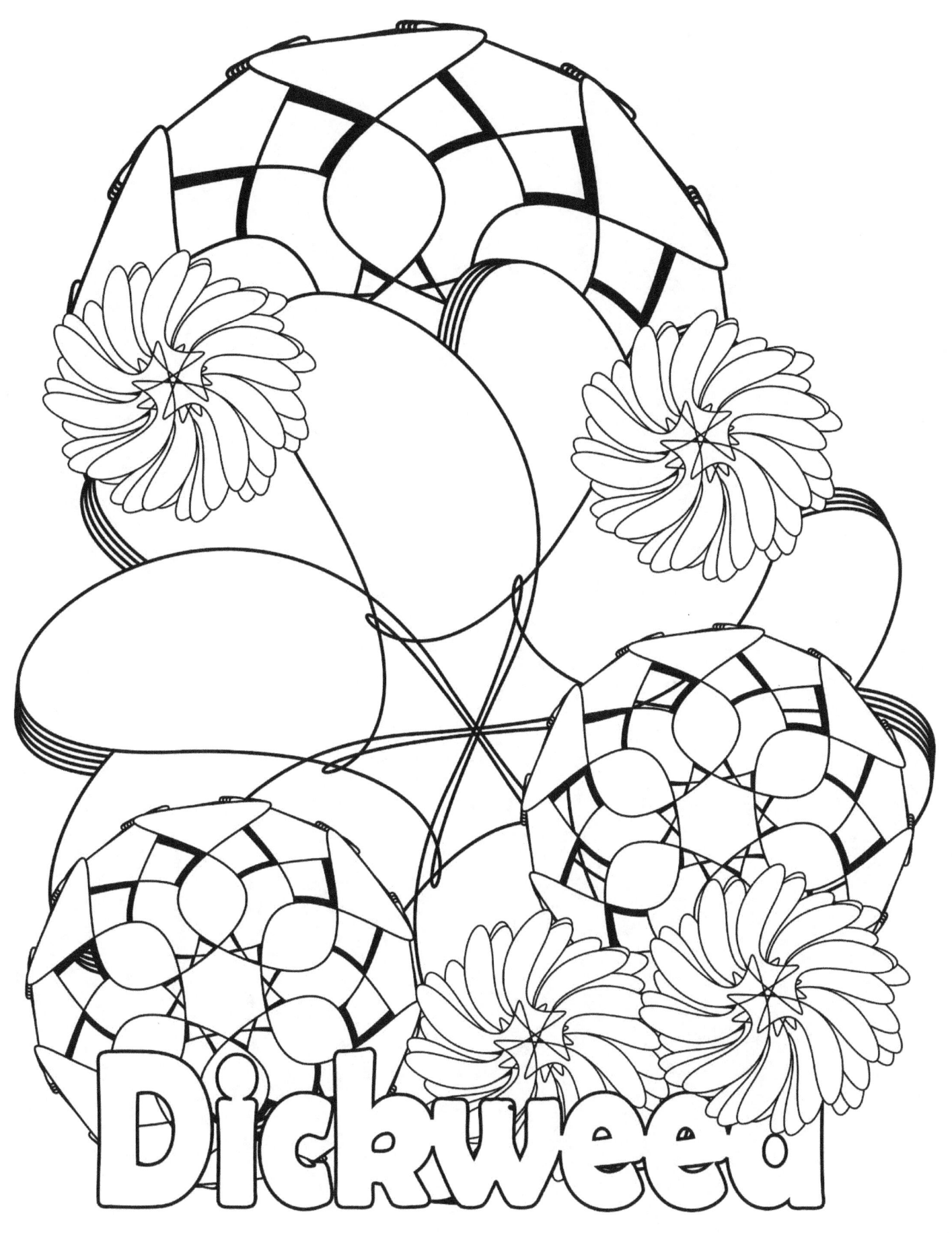

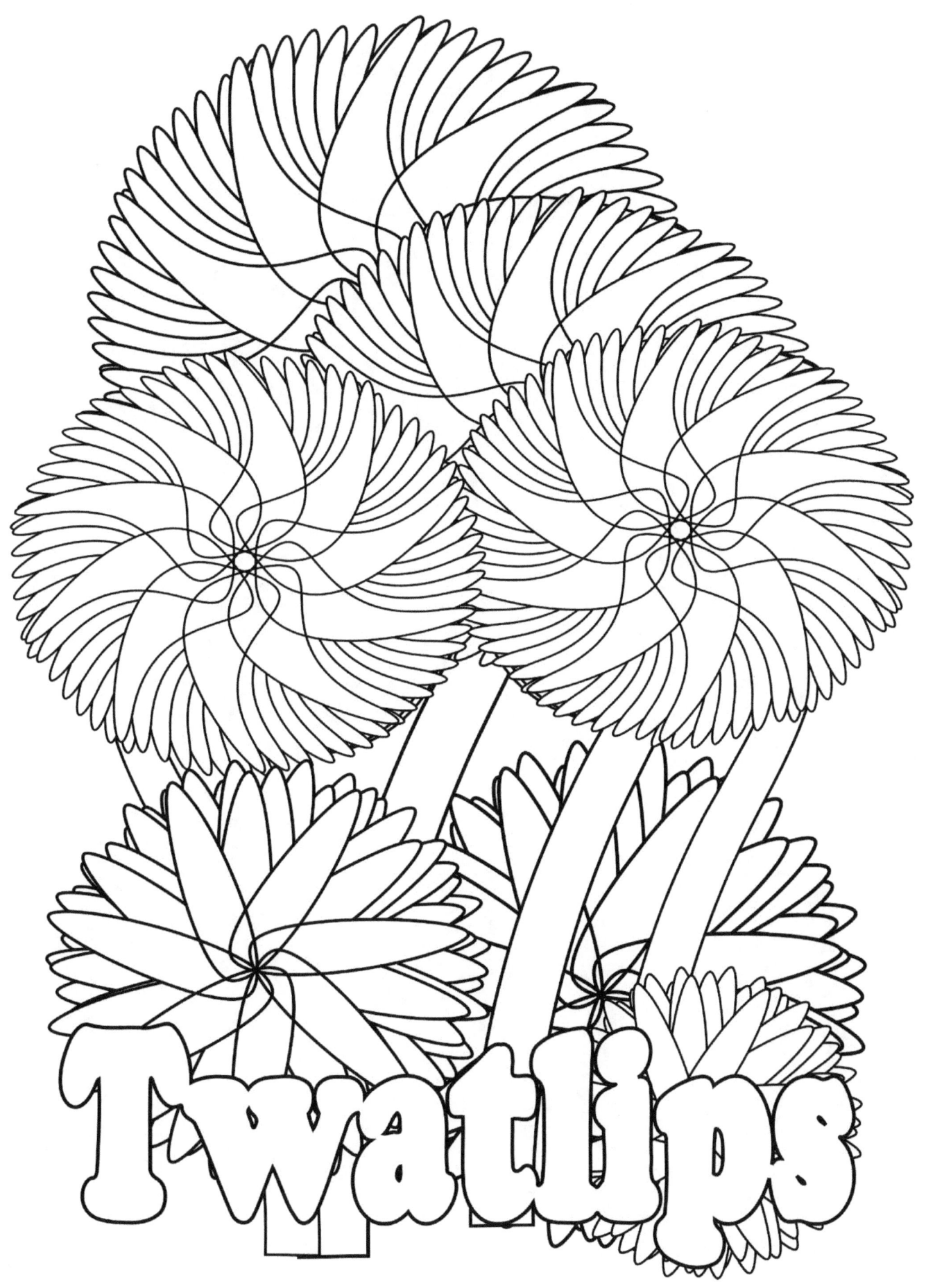

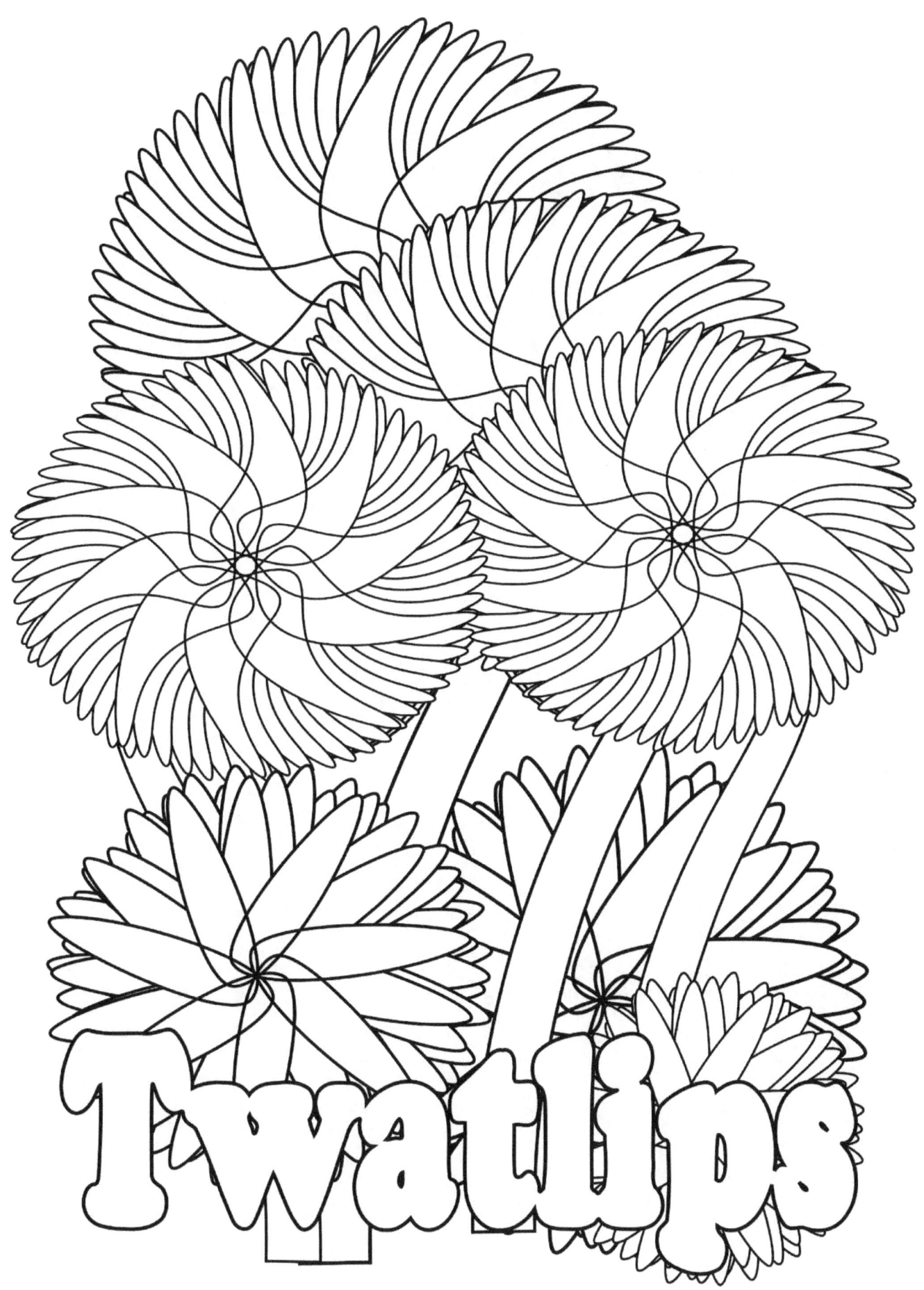

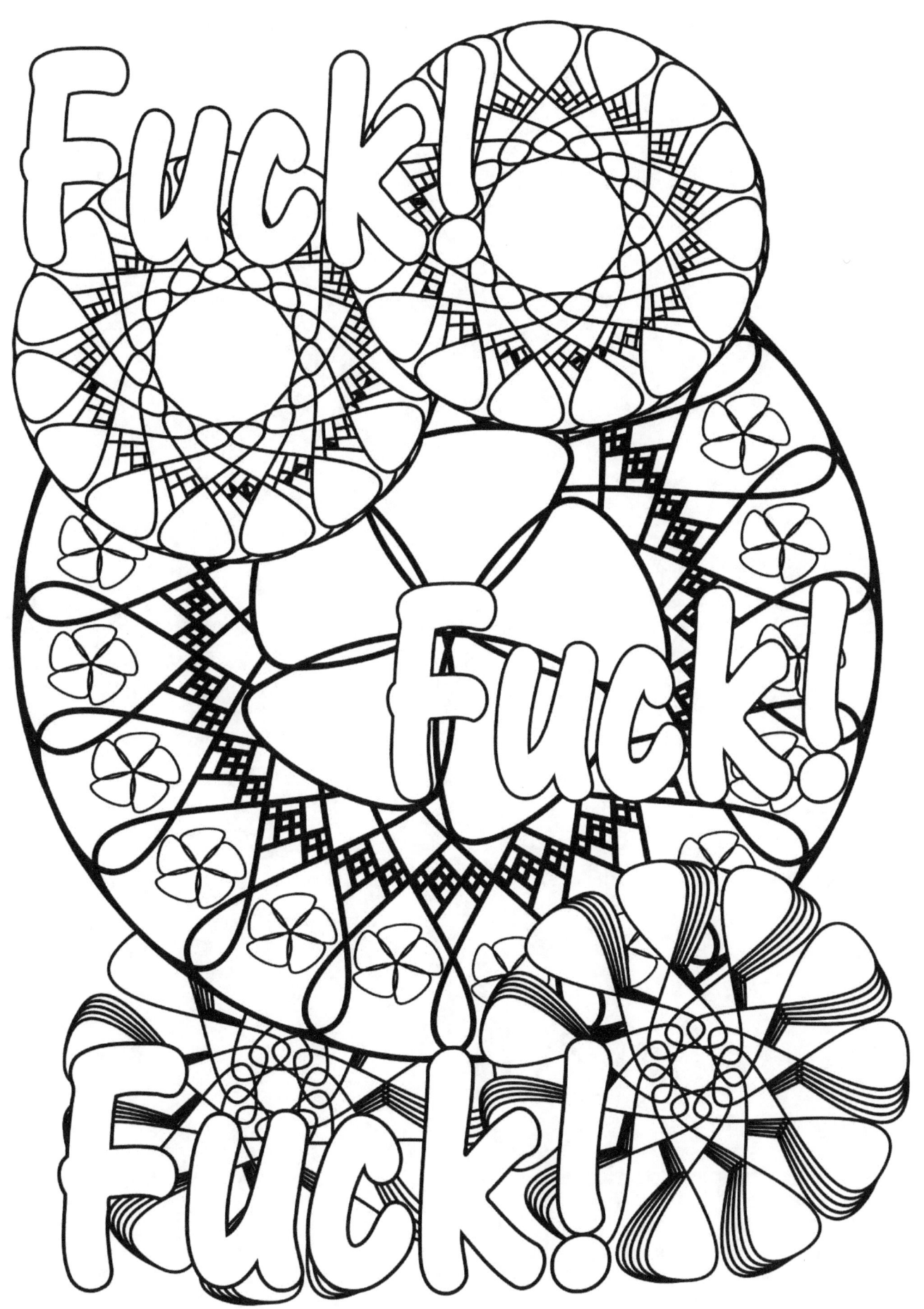

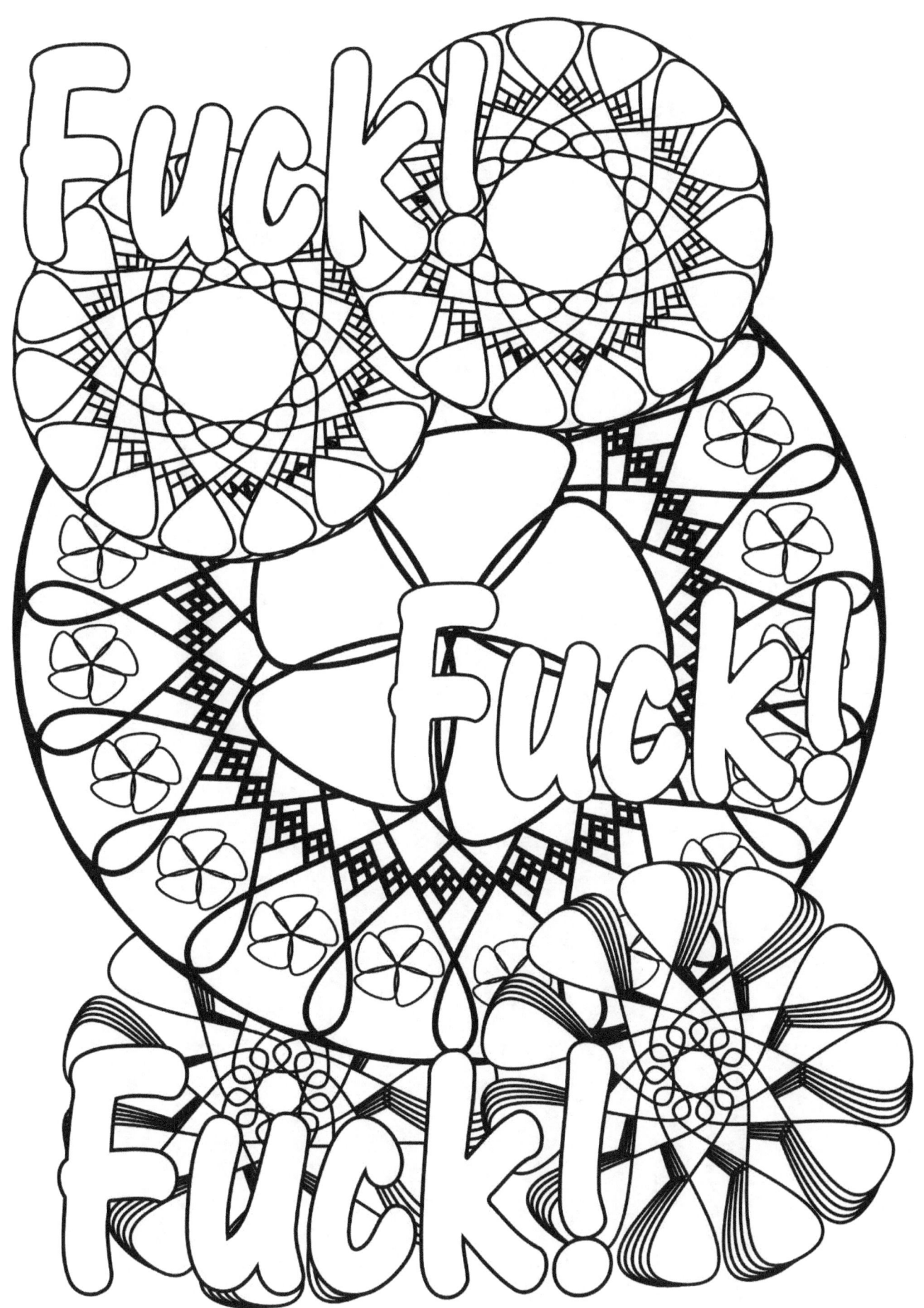

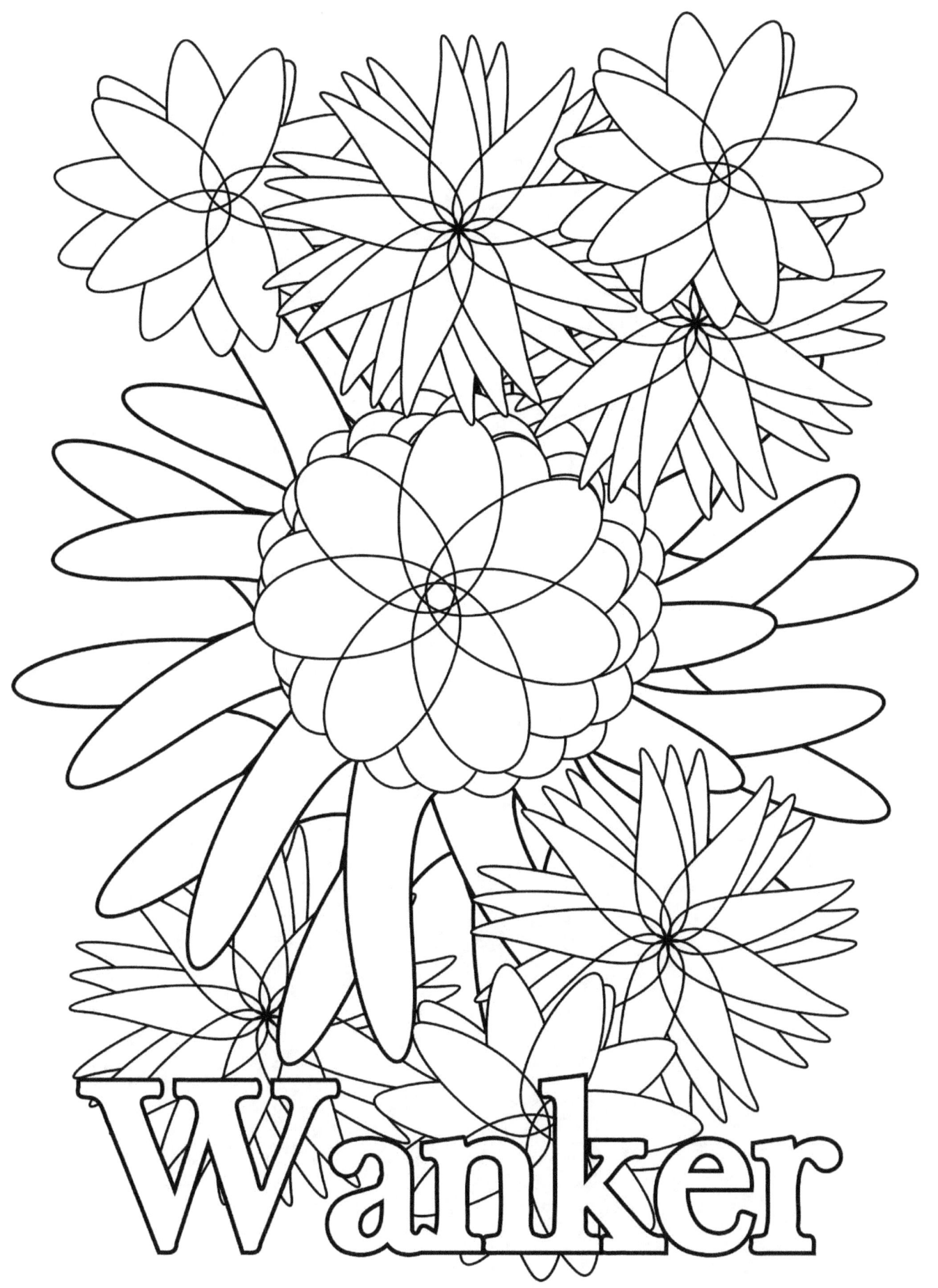

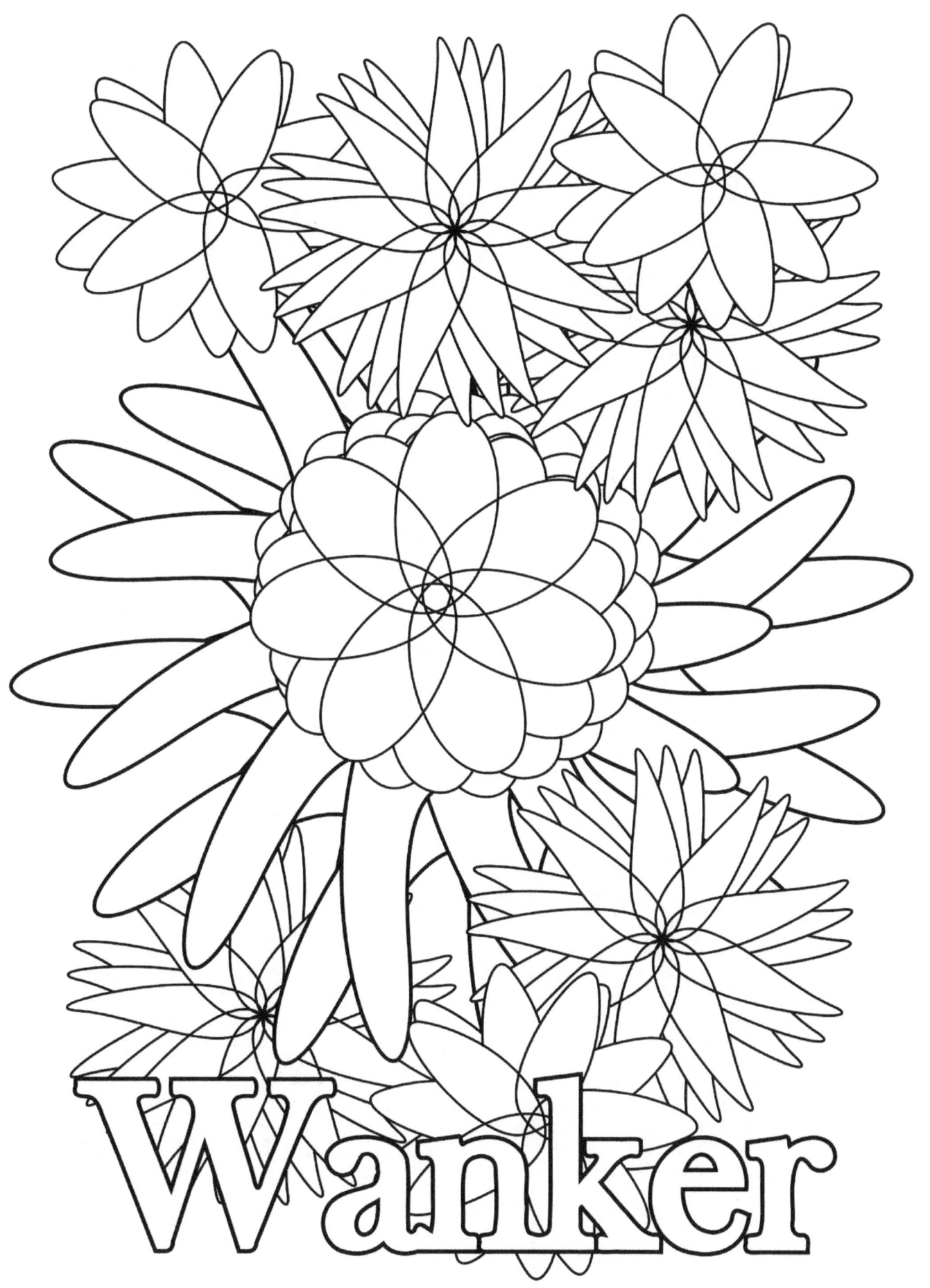

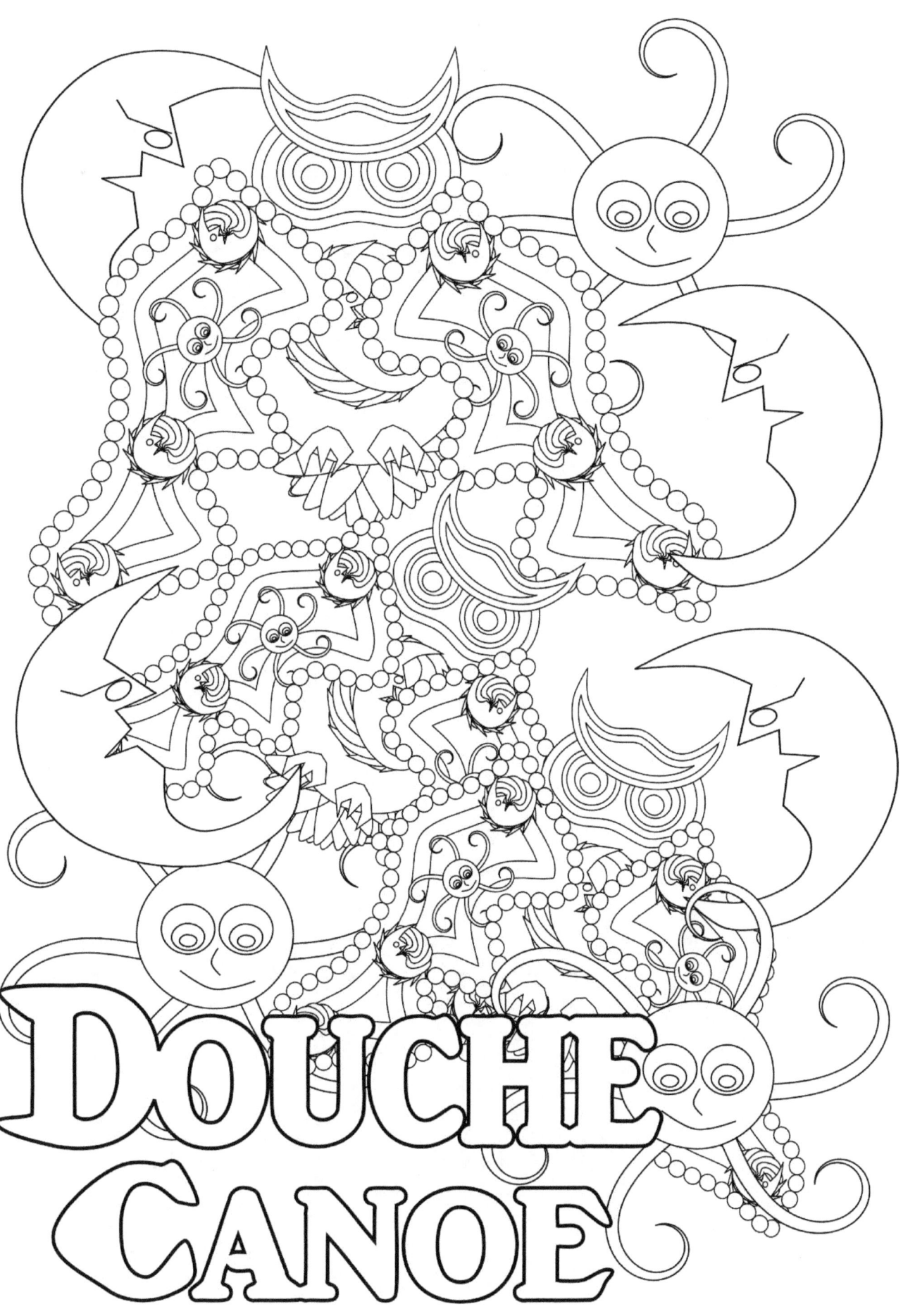

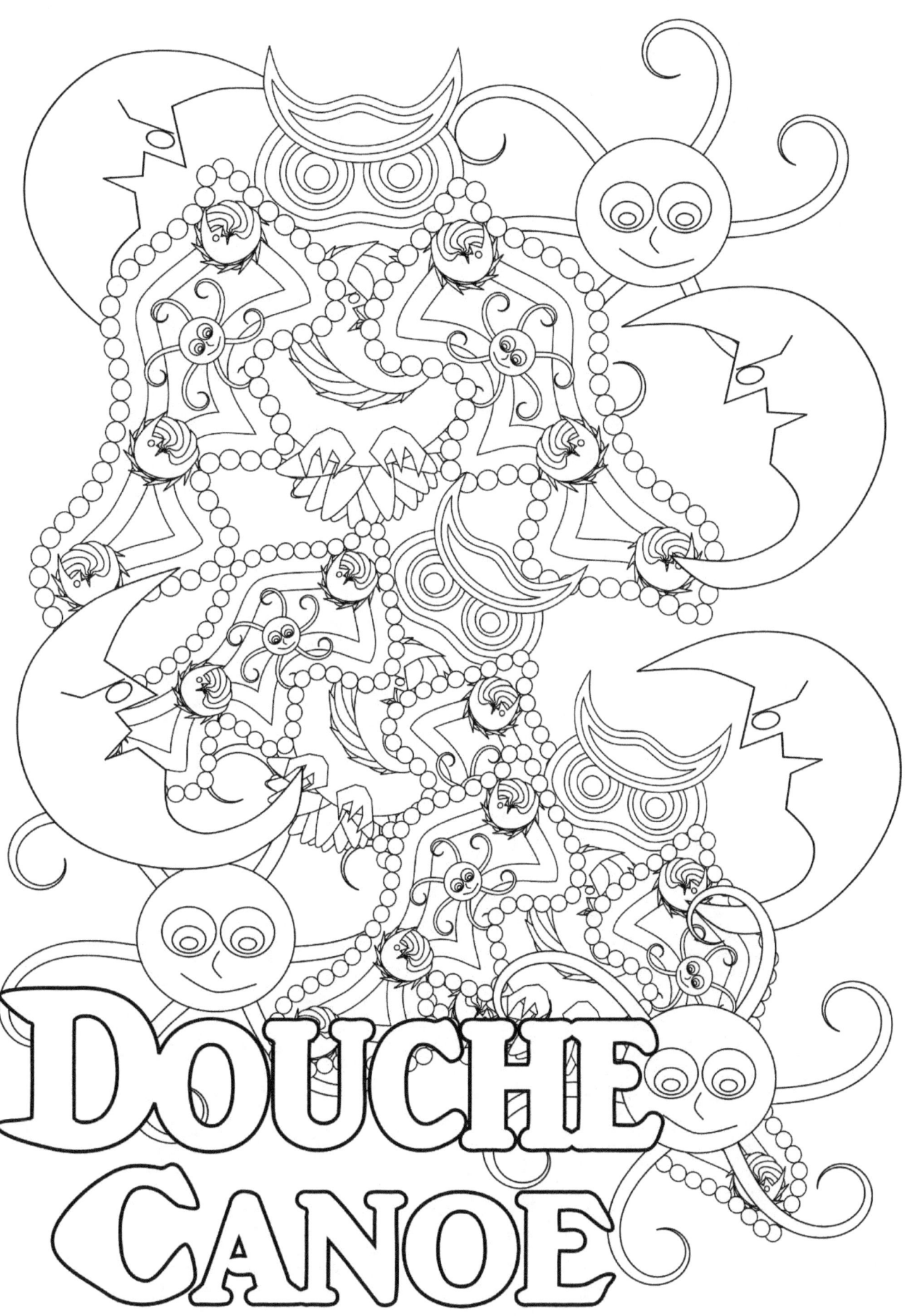

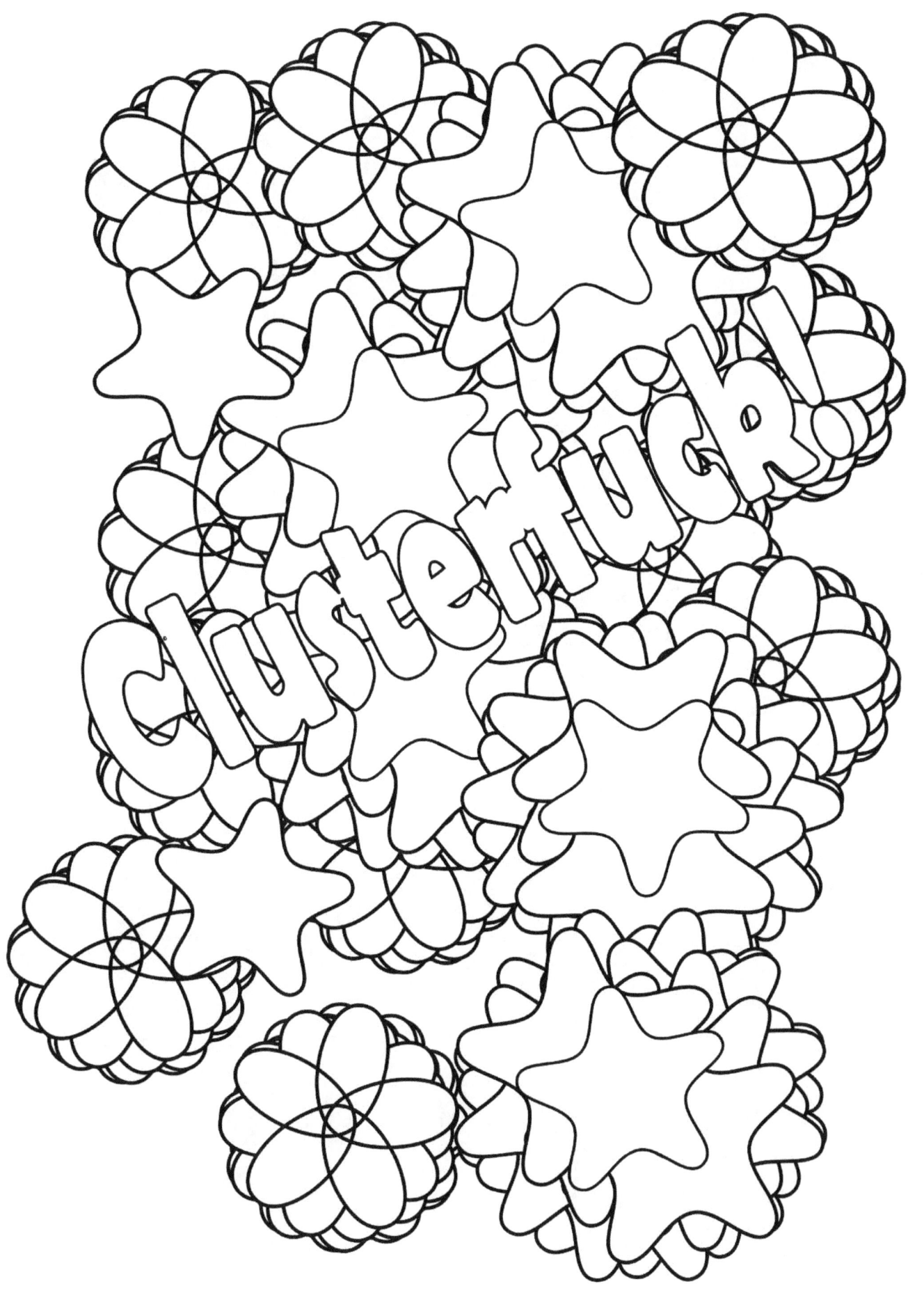

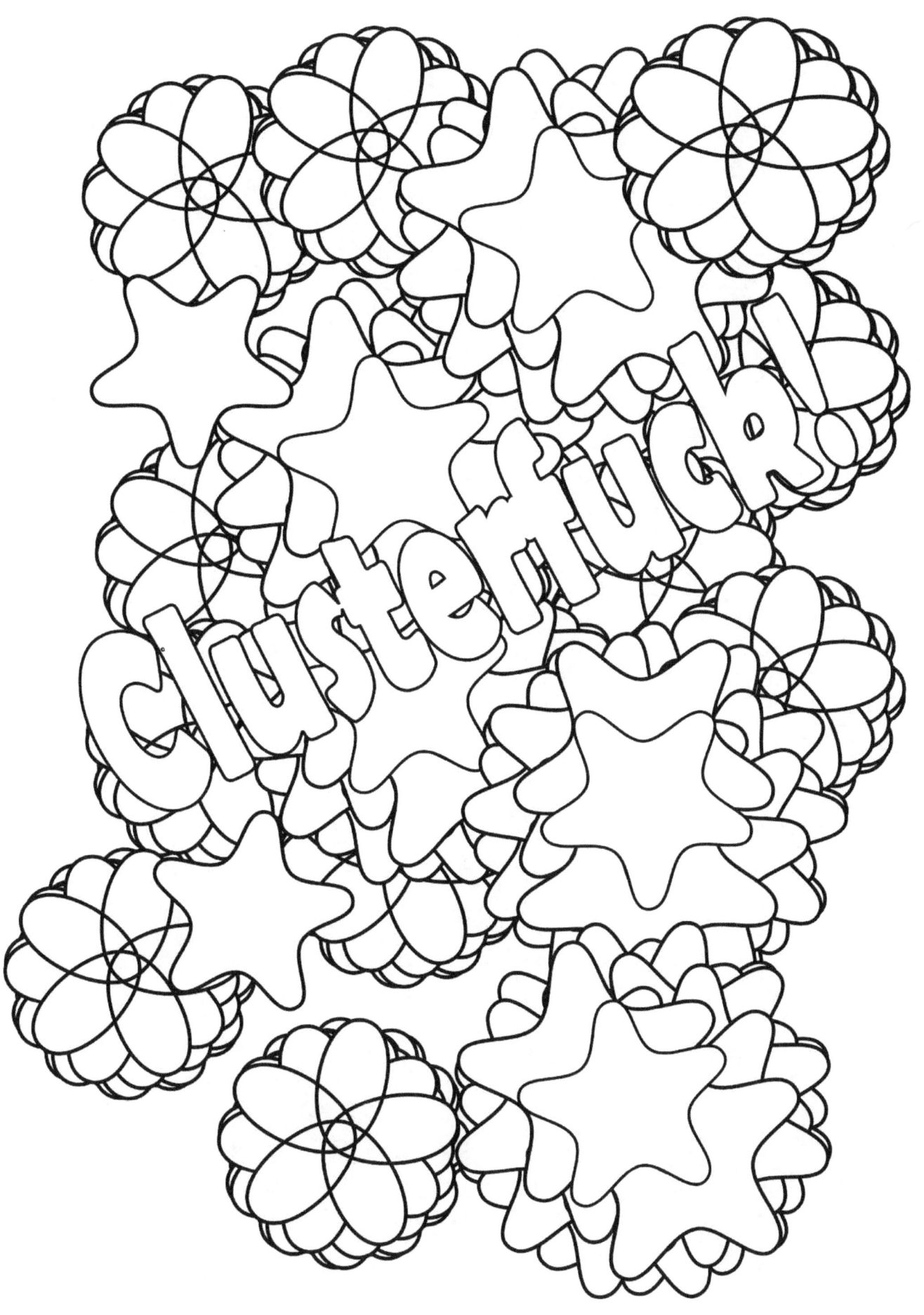

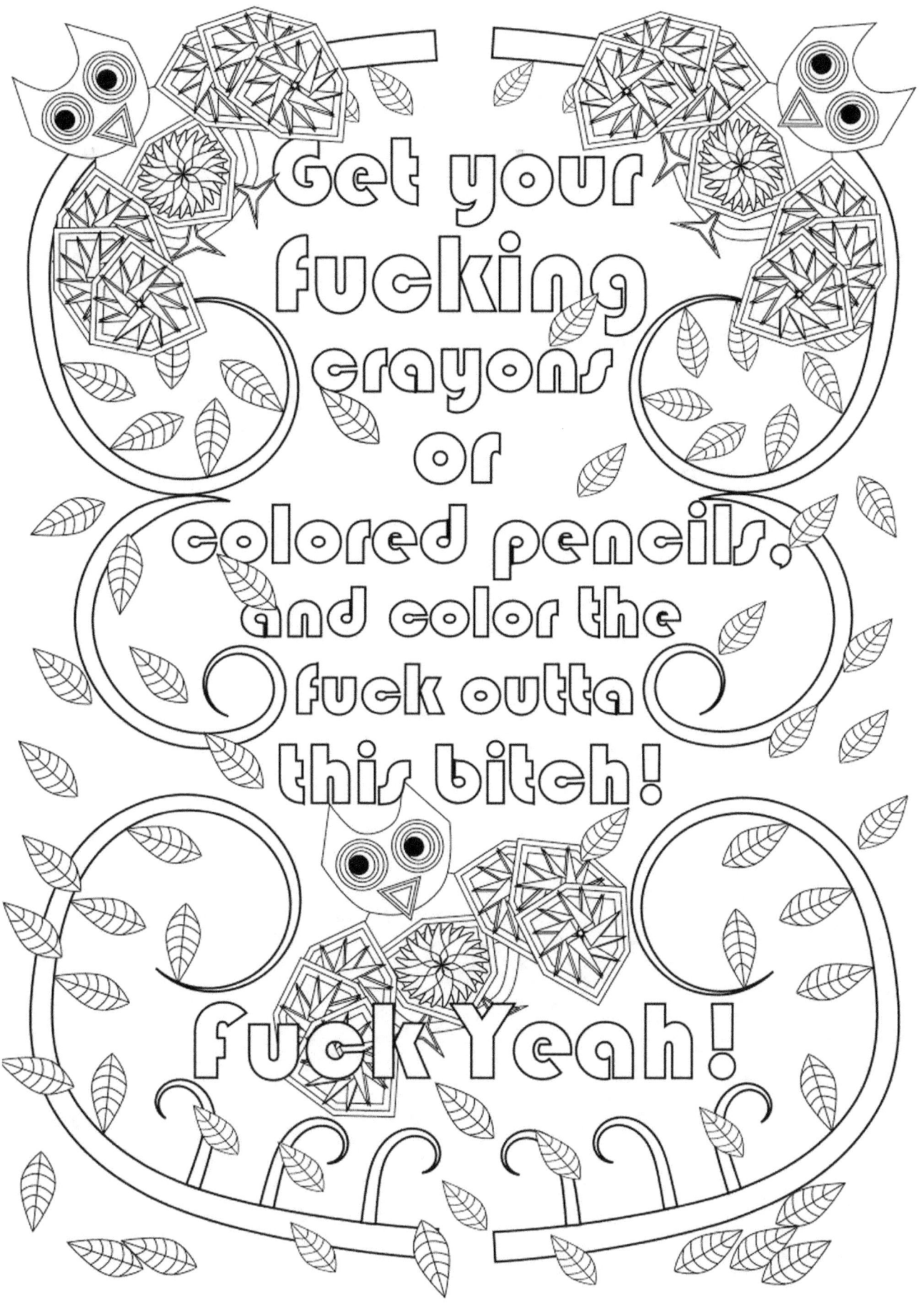

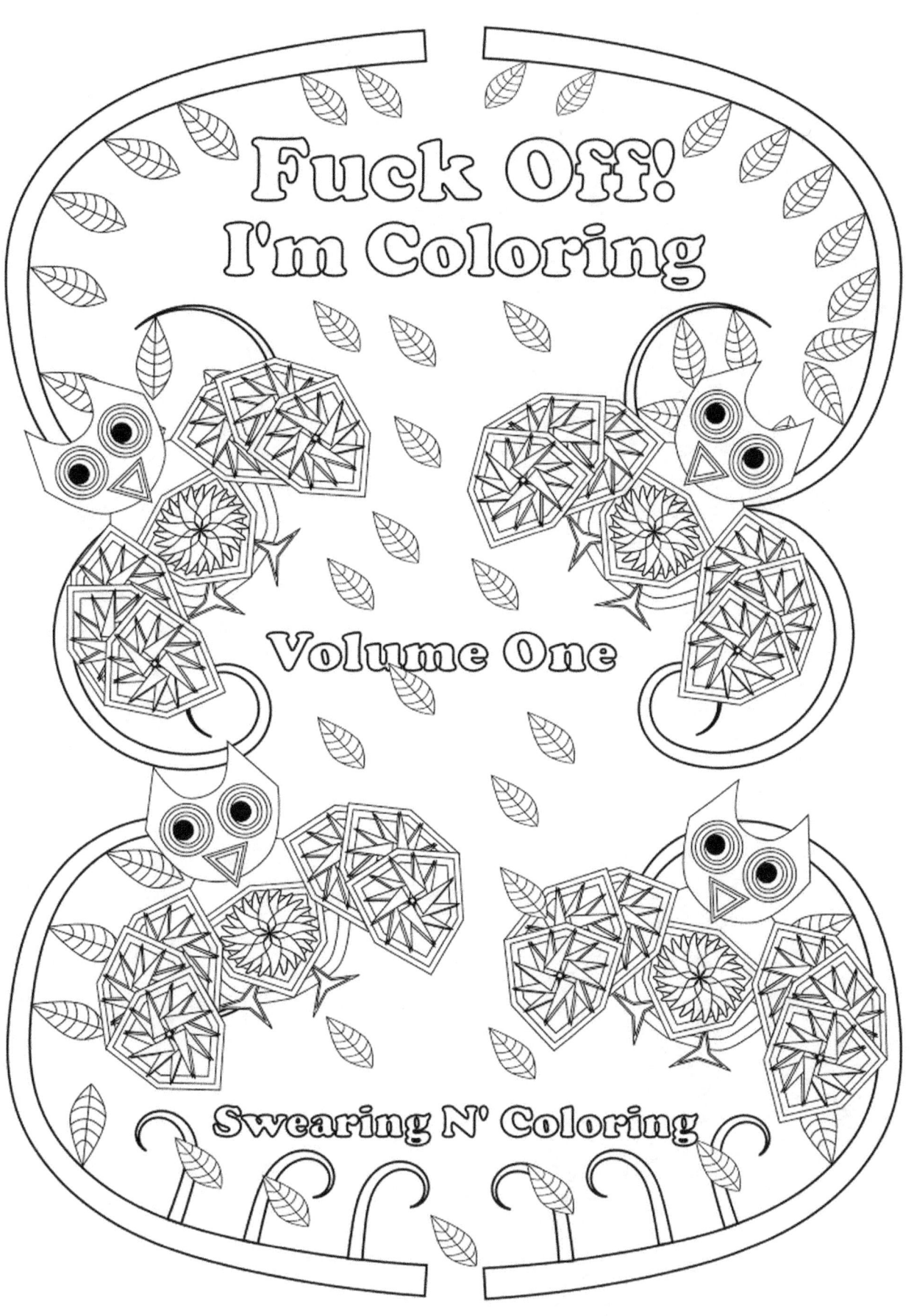

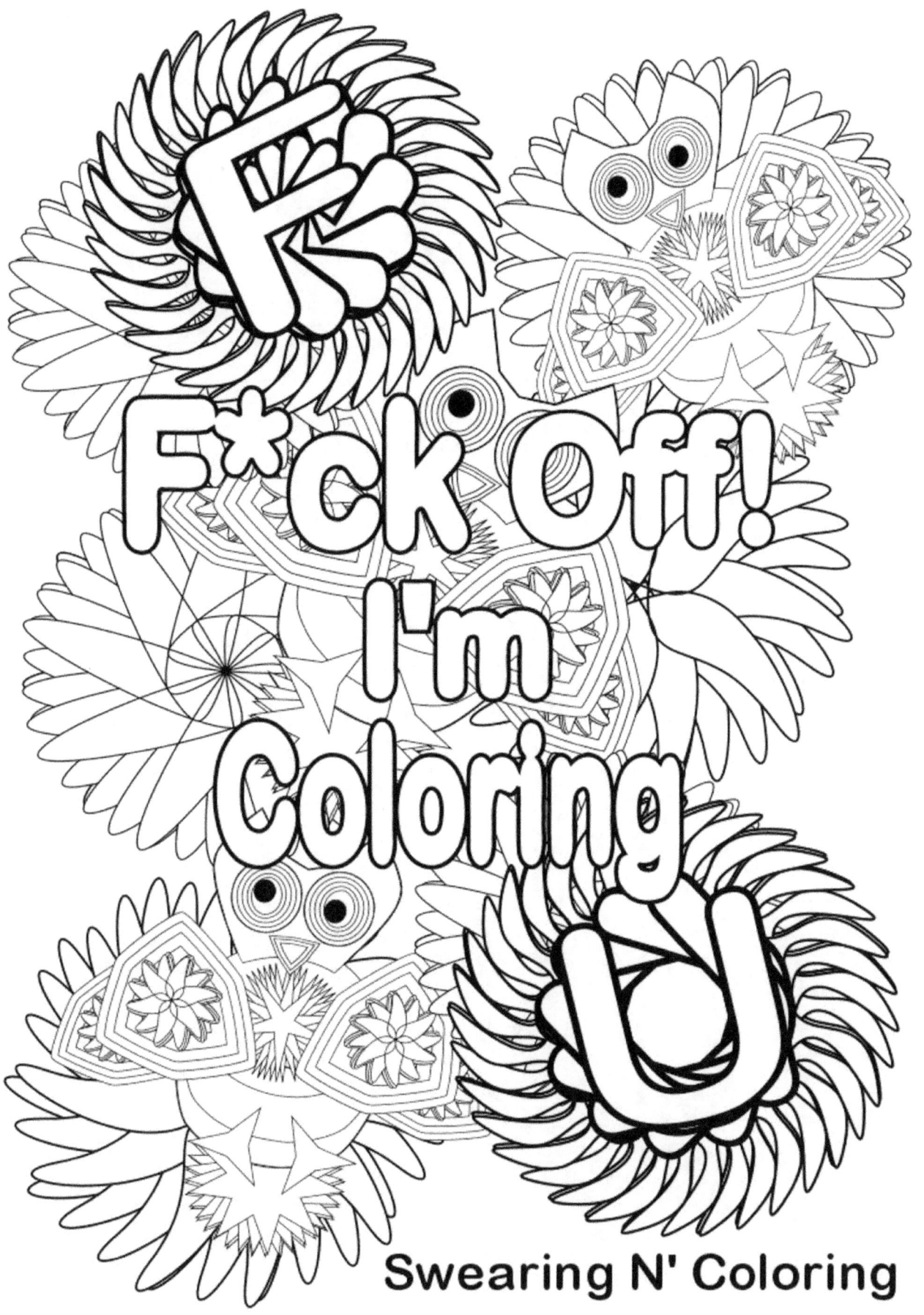

Swearing N' Coloring

www.ingramcontent.com/pod-product-compliance
Lightning Source LLC
Chambersburg PA
CBHW080706190526
45169CB00006B/2269